W9-ADE-862

The Atlantic Slave Trade

Florida A&M University, Tallahassee
Florida Atlantic University, Boca Raton
Florida Gulf Coast University, Ft. Myers
Florida International University, Miami
Florida State University, Tallahassee
University of Central Florida, Orlando
University of Florida, Gainesville
University of North Florida, Jacksonville
University of South Florida, Tampa
University of West Florida, Pensacola

The Atlantic Slave Trade

JOHANNES POSTMA

UNIVERSITY PRESS OF FLORIDA
Gainesville/Tallahassee/Tampa/Boca Raton
Pensacola/Orlando/Miami/Jacksonville/Ft. Myers

Copyright 2003 by Johannes Postma

First paperback printing 2005 by the University Press of Florida

Published in paperback by arrangement with Greenwood Publishing Group, Inc., Westport, Connecticut. All rights reserved.

No part of this book may be reproduced or transmitted in any form or by any means electronic or mechanical including photocopying, reprinting, or on any information storage or retrieval system, without a license or permission in writing from Greenwood Publishing Group. www.greenwood.com.

Printed in the United States of America on acid-free paper

10 09 08 07 06 05   6 5 4 3 2 1

A record of cataloging-in-publication data is available from the Library of Congress.

ISBN 0-8130-2906-6

The University Press of Florida is the scholarly publishing agency for the State University System of Florida, comprising Florida A&M University, Florida Atlantic University, Florida Gulf Coast University, Florida International University, Florida State University, University of Central Florida, University of Florida, University of North Florida, University of South Florida, and University of West Florida.

University Press of Florida
15 Northwest 15th Street
Gainesville, FL 32611–2079
http://www.upf.com

CONTENTS

ILLUSTRATIONS

SERIES FOREWORD

American statesman Adlai Stevenson stated, "We can chart our future clearly and wisely only when we know the path which has led to the present." This series, *Greenwood Guides to Historic Events 1500–1900,* is designed to illuminate that path by focusing on events from 1500 to 1900 that have shaped the world. These years include what historians call the Early Modern Period (1500 to 1789, the onset of the French Revolution) and part of the modern period (1789 to 1900).

In 1500, an acceleration of key trends marked the beginnings of an interdependent world and the posting of seminal questions that changed the nature and terms of intellectual debate. The series closes with 1900, the inauguration of the twentieth century. This period witnessed profound economic, social, political, cultural, religious, and military changes. An industrial and technological revolution transformed the modes of production, marked the transition from a rural to an urban economy, and ultimately raised the standard of living. Social classes and distinctions shifted. The emergence of the territorial and later the national state altered man's relations with and view of political authority. The shattering of the religious unity of the Roman Catholic world in Europe marked the rise of a new pluralism. Military revolutions changed the nature of warfare.

The books in this series emphasize the complexity and diversity of the human tapestry and include political, economic, social, intellectual, military, and cultural topics. Some of the authors focus on events in U.S. history, such as the Salem witchcraft trials, the American Revolution, the abolitionist movement, and the Civil War. Others analyze European topics, such as the Reformation and Counter Reformation and the French Revolution. Still others bridge cultures and continents by examining the voyages of discovery, the Atlantic slave trade, and the Age of Imperialism. Some focus on intellectual questions that have shaped the modern world, such as Darwin's *Origin of Species,* or on turning points such as the Age of Romanticism. Others examine defining economic, religious, or legal events or issues such as the building of the railroads, the Second Great Awakening, and abolitionism. Heroes (e.g., Lewis and Clark), scientists (e.g., Darwin), military leaders (e.g., Napoleon), poets (e.g., Byron), stride across its pages. Many of these events were seminal in that they marked profound changes or turning points. The scientific revolution, for example, changed the way individuals viewed themselves and their world.

The authors, acknowledged experts in their fields, synthesize key events, set developments within the larger historical context, and, most importantly, present a well-balanced, well-written account that integrates the most recent scholarship in the field.

An advisory board composed of historians, high school history teachers, and school librarians chose the topics to support the curriculum and meet student research needs. The volumes are designed to serve as resources for student research and to provide clearly written interpretations of topics central to the secondary school and lower-level undergraduate history curriculum. Each author outlines a basic chronology to guide the reader through often confusing events and a historical overview to set those events within a narrative framework. Three to five topical chapters underscore critical aspects of the event. In the final chapter, the author examines the impact and consequences of the event. Biographical sketches furnish background on the lives and contributions of the players who strut across this stage. Ten to fifteen primary documents ranging from letters to diary entries, song lyrics, proclamations, and posters, cast light on the event, provide material for student essays, and stimulate a critical engagement with the sources. Introductions identify the authors of the documents and the main issues. In some cases, a glossary of selected terms is provided as a guide to the reader. Each work contains an annotated bibliography of recommended books, articles, CD-ROMs, Internet sites, videos, and films that set the materials within the historical debate.

These works will lead to a more sophisticated understanding of the events and debates that have shaped the modern world and will stimulate a more active engagement with the issues that still affect us. It has been a particularly enriching experience to work closely with such dedicated professionals. We have come to know and value even more highly the authors in this series and our editors at Greenwood, particularly Barbara Rader and Kevin Ohe. In many cases, they have become more than colleagues; they have become friends. To them and to future historians we dedicate this series.

Linda S. Frey
University of Montana

Marsha L. Frey
Kansas State University

PREFACE

The slave trade from Africa to the Americas was the largest forced migration in human history. This heartrending chapter of our times has been long ignored, but it demands attention when studying world history. The slaves were rarely able to record their experiences, although a few narratives written by them have survived and are included with the primary documents in this publication.

This book attempts to explain the circumstances under which the African diaspora occurred, from the moment of enslavement in Africa, through the dreaded Middle Passage, and to the disembarkation and sale of the slaves in the Americas. Utilizing surviving contemporary accounts left by the enslaved, slave traders, and a variety of other sources, and particularly the wealth of archival research conducted during the past three decades, it is possible to get a better understanding of what happened in the slave trade and why.

The role of historians is to restructure an image of the past that corresponds as closely with reality as possible. New generations invariably ask new questions that lead to new searches and new explanations. Hence, history will repeatedly need to be rewritten. We must be careful, however, that we judge the past in terms of its own realities and values, and not by our present-day society and its ideals.

ACKNOWLEDGMENTS

Several years of archival research and participation in professional conferences about the slave trade provided the foundation for writing this book. Teaching college classes on slavery and the slave trade for many years gave me the confidence to accept the task. Although this has been essentially a solitary endeavor, many people have contributed indirectly to it, either through their publications or through discussions and correspondence.

In particular, I want to thank Herbert Klein, who recently wrote his own history of the Atlantic slave trade, for his valuable advice and suggestions. I also want to thank the editors of the *Greenwood Guides to Historic Events 1500–1900,* Marsha L. Frey and Linda S. Frey, for their support and constructive editorial suggestions. Kevin Ohe, editor for the series at Greenwood Press, has been most helpful with editorial advice and the production process. The staff of Impressions Book and Journal Services and copy editor Fran Lyon have made a valuable contribution by polishing and synchronizing the contents of the manuscript. Above all, I want to thank my wife, Joelle Million, who shared the anxiety involved in writing a book and took time from her own writing projects to read and edit every part of this publication.

The libraries of the University of Massachusetts at Amherst, Smith College, and Amherst College, particularly its Special Collection Division, have been valuable sources of information. Their personnel were very courteous and helpful.

Credit is due to several publishers who generously permitted republication of primary documents: Cambridge University Press,

Carnegie Institution of Washington, Frank Cass Publishers, Waveland Press, and Heinemann Publishers. The Archéologie Navale Classique Recherche Édition (ANCRE), The Hakluyt Society, Johns Hopkins University Press, University of Wisconsin Press, the Historisch Museum at Rotterdam, and Corbis-Bettmann granted permissions for illustrations.

CHRONOLOGY OF EVENTS

1441   Africans enslaved by Portuguese sailors on the coast of Mauritania

1444   Portuguese trading expeditions with Africa start; slaves are bought, kidnapped, and taken to Lisbon

1479   Portugal and Spain sign Treaty of Aláçvas; Portugal to supply Spain with slaves

1482   Portuguese start to build trading castle São Jorge da Mina at Elmina, which remains their West African headquarters till 1637

1492   Columbus's first visit to the Americas

1494   First Africans travel as free men with Columbus to Caribbean island of Hispaniola

1494   Treaty of Tordesillas gives Portugal monopoly over Africa, and Spain over America with the exception of Brazil

1502   First African slaves brought to Hispaniola

1510   First large transport of 250 African slaves from Lisbon to the New World

1528   First *asiento* (contract), starting the slave traffic directly from Africa to the Americas

1542   Spain abolishes Amerindian slavery and the *encomienda* system

1550   First small slave shipments directly from Africa to Brazil

1562–63   John Hawkins's first English slaving voyages across the Atlantic

1595	Spanish Crown renews slave trade *asiento*
1619	Twenty African slaves brought by a Dutch ship to Jamestown, Virginia
1625	The English acquire Barbados and start cultivating sugar on the island
1630	The Dutch capture northern Brazil and establish New Holland colony
1634	The Dutch capture Curaçao and make it a slave trade depot in the 1650s
1637	Dutch fleet captures the Portuguese headquarters at Elmina and maintain it until 1872
1655	Jamaica settled by the English, who develop it into a major sugar-growing island
1667	The Dutch capture Surinam from the English, and keep it in return for New Amsterdam (New York) in a negotiated settlement with England that same year
1730s	First Maroon wars at Jamaica
1760s	Maroons in Surinam gain their independence, negotiating treaties with Dutch authorities
1763–64	Rebelling slaves almost gain control of the Dutch colony of Berbice (in today's Guyana)
1770	Abbé Raynal publishes book, *Histoire philosophique,* condemning slavery
1772	British Chief Justice Lord Mansfield rules in Somerset case that slavery has its limits in Britain, but is not illegal, as is often assumed
1775	Pennsylvania Abolition Society is organized
1776	British and American Quakers require their members to free their slaves
1777	Vermont Constitution makes slavery illegal
1778	British Parliament creates committee to investigate the Atlantic slave trade
1783	Interpretation of Massachusetts Constitution makes slavery illegal in the state

1783   Quakers petition British Parliament and U.S. Congress to end the slave trade

1784   Gradual emancipation laws are adopted in Rhode Island and Connecticut

1787   The Society for the Abolition of the Slave Trade is established in London

1787   U.S. Constitutional Convention agrees not to end the slave trade before 1808

1787   Rhode Island's citizens are forbidden to take part in the slave trade

1788   The Société des Amis des Noirs (Friends of the Blacks) is established in Paris

1788   Dolben Act, regulating conditions aboard slave ships, adopted by British Parliament

1788   The citizens of Connecticut, New York, Massachusetts, and Pennsylvania are no longer allowed to engage in the slave trade

1788   The Sierra Leone Company is organized to promote settlements of free blacks in Africa

1789   Twelve resolutions against the slave trade are introduced in Parliament by William Wilberforce

1790   Mulatto uprising starts in St. Domingue, led by Vincent Ogé

1791   Massive slave revolt in St. Domingue leads to the independence of Haiti by 1804

1792   British House of Commons passes law to end slave trade, but House of Lords vetoes it

1792   Popular boycott against the use of slave-grown sugar gains support in Britain

1792   Denmark ends participation in the Atlantic slave trade, to be effective by 1803

1792   Black American refugees in Nova Scotia are taken to Sierra Leone

1793   Eli Whitney invents the cotton gin, which spreads slavery westward in southern states

1794	The French National Convention outlaws slavery in the colonies
1794	First delegate convention of state abolition societies meets in Philadelphia
1798	Georgia is the last state of the Union to prohibit the importation of slaves
1799	British Parliament passes new restrictions for slave accommodations on slave ships
1800	Gabriel Prosser's plot to capture Richmond is foiled
1802	Napoleon repeals the law of 1794 and reinstates slavery in France's colonies
1802	Toussaint L'Ouverture unifies the island of Hispaniola and becomes governor for life, but is captured that same year and taken to France as a prisoner
1803	Jacques Dessalines proclaims the independence of Haiti, and the French army withdraws
1804	Slavery abolished in Haiti
1806	British Parliament passes law prohibiting British slave trade to foreign markets
1806	President Jefferson urges the end of the U.S. slave trade after 1807
1807	Parliament passes law that prohibits British subjects to engage in the slave trade, or to import slaves to British possessions after May 1, 1807
1807	U.S. Congress prohibits Americans from engaging in the Atlantic slave trade by January 1, 1808
1810	British treaty with Portugal to restrict the latter's slave trade
1810	Unsuccessful attempts in Venezuela and Mexico to abolish the slave trade
1813	Argentina starts gradual emancipation of slaves
1814	The Kingdom of the Netherlands ends its participation in the Atlantic slave trade
1815	Napoleon abolishes the French slave trade, and his Bourbon successors adopt an ineffective prohibition of the traffic

1815	The international Congress of Vienna condemns the slave trade as inhumane
1816	Latin American liberators Simón Bolívar and José de San Martín offer slaves their freedom if they join the war of liberation against Spain
1816	The American Colonization Society is established and encourages emigration of free Blacks to Africa
1817	Portugal and Spain agree to end the slave trade north of the equator
1819	The British navy establishes anti-slave-trade squadron for West Africa
1819	Parliament passes a law that requires the registration of slaves in the British colonies, a move toward the emancipation of slavery
1820	The U.S. Congress declares that participation in the slave trade is equivalent to piracy
1821	Peru and Colombia take steps to end the slave trade and slavery
1822	A British attempt to create an international police force to suppress the slave trade fails
1823	Anti-Slavery Committee is established in London
1823	Slave rebellion planned by Denmark Vesey is uncovered
1823	Chile adopts a law for general emancipation
1823	A major slave rebellion in Demerara (British Guyana)
1823–24	Slavery is abolished in Chile and Central America
1826	Spain and Portugal promise Britain to end their slave trade by 1830
1829	Slavery is abolished in Mexico
1831	Nat Turner's slave rebellion in Virginia
1833	American Abolition Society founded in Philadelphia
1835	Anglo-Spanish treaty is ineffective in ending the slave trade to Cuba
1834–38	Slavery is abolished throughout the British Empire
1841	The Quintuple Treaty between Britain, France, Russia, Prussia, and Austria allows mutual searches at sea, in order to combat illegal slave trade

CHAPTER 1

FORCED MIGRATION FROM AFRICA: AN OVERVIEW

Civilization and Slavery

Various forms of servitude have existed since humans started using domesticated plants and animals approximately eight to ten thousand years ago, when hunting and gathering was gradually replaced by settled life in villages and towns. The new lifestyle offered several advantages, including surplus food and increased population. In time, large and complex states emerged that were governed from urban centers. Groups of specialists surfaced, including kings, aristocrats, priests, soldiers, and scholars, who enjoyed exceptional privileges. The Greeks called it civilization. But specialization also created servile groups, who were dominated by others and forced to perform harsh and undesirable tasks for little or no reward. At the very bottom of the social structure were people who lost their freedom altogether. They were slaves.

The institution of slavery has been a common feature of many societies from ancient times to the present. It was a worldwide phenomenon, known by different names and marked by varying degrees of exploitation. As historian Orlando Patterson states:

> There is nothing peculiar about the institution of slavery. It has existed from before the dawn of human history right down to the twentieth century, in the most primitive of human societies and in the most civilized. There is no region on earth that has not at some time harbored the institution. Probably there is no group of people whose ancestors were not at one time slaves or slave holders.[1]

In the much-admired European societies of Greece and Rome, slaves sometimes comprised half of the population. Slavery was widespread in the Byzantine Empire (ca. 500–1500), the successor state of the Roman Empire in southeastern Europe and the Middle East, as well as in the Turkish Ottoman Empire (ca. 1300–1800) in the Middle East and North Africa. The slave markets of Venice, in today's Italy, sold more than ten thousand slaves in the years 1414–23, before slaves from tropical Africa were shipped to Europe.[2]

Dimensions of Servitude

Another word for servitude is bondage, which means that persons are bound or forced to provide service to their masters. Various degrees of bondage have existed in human history, as illustrated below. From left to right, each condition increases in severity.

Vassals—Pawns—Indentures—Serfs—Slaves—Chattel Slaves

Vassals were bound by mutual obligation to members of the upper class, or aristocracy. Pawns were temporarily enslaved to guarantee a business agreement. Indentured servants were obligated to serve a master for a contracted number of years, after which they were free. Serfs were bound to the land, had limited freedom, and had to work for their masters, but they also had the right to marry, hold personal property, own a plot of land, and be members of a church and village. Though serfs were rarely sold, their lives were often brutal, and their social superiors viewed them with contempt. Slavery came in various forms, depending on the wealth and occupation of the slave's master and the climate, traditions, and laws of the region. In most cases, a slave was a stranger who had no roots or family in the community where he or she was forced to reside. Chattel slavery represented the most severe form of servitude. It deprived the subject of all rights and allowed the owner to punish and sell the slave at will. Such slaves were considered the property, or the chattel (capital), of the owner. Historian Paul Lovejoy defines chattel slavery as follows:

> Its special characteristics included the idea that slaves were property; that they were outsiders who were alien by origin or who had been denied their heritage . . . ; that coercion could be used at will; that their labor power was at the complete disposal of the master; that they did not have the right to their own sexuality and, by extension, to their own reproductive capacities; and that the slave

status was inherited unless provision was made to ameliorate that status.[3]

Slavery was most common in large and centrally controlled societies, and enslavement tended to increase in times of warfare. Expanding empires often captured many prisoners of war, who were enslaved and put to work in mines and on rural estates. As territorial expansion diminished, fewer captives were taken, and the offspring of slaves gradually merged into society with greater privileges than their enslaved ancestors. This process occurred in Europe when the Roman Empire declined. As medieval Europe (ca. 500–1500 C.E.) settled into a more self-sufficient agricultural society, slavery gradually changed into serfdom. In southern and eastern Europe, slavery lingered and slave markets continued to operate in such towns as Lisbon, Seville, Genoa, and Antwerp until the seventeenth century. Slavery continued to thrive in many societies throughout the world.

Most slaves remained bound for life, and their children inherited their inferior status. In some societies, however, highly gifted and ambitious slaves could occasionally advance to influential positions, as the biblical story of Joseph illustrates. Through skill and good luck, Joseph climbed to the highest political position under the Egyptian pharaoh. In the thirteenth century, a former slave named Sakura managed to rise to the leadership of the army in the West African empire of Mali and eventually became its ruler.

These incidents illustrate that slavery existed in Africa as well as in Europe. Africa experienced the same social evolution that accompanied the agricultural revolution in other parts of the world. Most African societies had various types of servitude, from harsh slavery to institutions similar to serfdom.[4] But neither African nor European slavery was based on race. Greeks, Romans, and other imperialists enslaved people of various defeated ethnic groups as their empires expanded. A wide variety of ethnic, religious, and racial minorities comprised the slave communities of early modern Spain, Portugal, and Italy. As Portuguese traders increased their contacts with sub-Saharan Africa, slaves from that region increased, but also among them were Moors (Muslims) from North Africa and European convicts. European sailors were enslaved in large numbers in North Africa.[5] Sugar plantations on Mediterranean islands, such as Sicily, used slaves shipped from the Black Sea region in today's

Russia and Ukraine. Slavic or Slavonic peoples were commonly enslaved in what was known as the "great Mediterranean slave trade," which reached its peak during the fourteenth and fifteenth centuries. Many eastern European and Christian slaves were sold to Saracen merchants at this time and were shipped to North Africa. The words Slavic and slave are derived from the same Latin root, *sclava*.[6]

More than One African Diaspora

The African continent has an enormous diversity of cultures and languages, and a captivating history. Long before the Atlantic slave trade, Africa had highly developed states, such as ancient Ghana, Mali, and Songhay in the west; Egypt and Ethiopia in the northeast; and Lunda in the south-central region. During the Atlantic slave trade, most people of sub-Saharan Africa were farmers. There were also nomadic and seminomadic pastoral societies that specialized in cattle herding, and until recently a few communities maintained a hunter-gatherer lifestyle. Yet commerce, including long-distance trade, played an important role throughout the continent. Both western and eastern Africa exported gold for many centuries. Large caravan routes crossed the Sahara Desert for more than a millennium, transporting gold, salt, and other products, as well as slaves. East Africa had commercial contacts across the Indian Ocean for many centuries.

One of the most troubling aspects of African history has been the forced migration of millions of its people, the so-called African diaspora, or out-migration. This diaspora was not limited to the transatlantic slave trade. Long before Africans were first taken to the Americas in the sixteenth century, there had been forced migration from sub-Saharan Africa to North Africa. Going back to the seventh century and continuing through most of the nineteenth, an estimated 9.4 million Africans were enslaved and forced to cross the Sahara Desert on foot to various North African destinations. An estimated 25 percent of these slaves either died during the crossing or were retained in desert-edge or oasis communities. Many ended up as soldiers in the slave armies of Egypt and Morocco, where they gradually assimilated in the mixed population of North Africa. During the same time, an estimated five million Africans were shipped across the Red Sea to Arabia and across the Indian Ocean to various destinations in southern and western Asia.[7]

Sugar and Slaves

During Europe's Middle Ages, sugar cultivation gradually spread from the Middle East to several Mediterranean islands. Because growing and processing sugar required a disciplined labor force, especially during the harvesting season, the use of forced labor became a virtual necessity. After the Iberians spread sugar cultivation to the Atlantic islands of Cape Verde, Madeira, and the Canaries, the Spanish enslaved and shipped aboriginal people from the Canary Islands to the Madeiras to work on the sugar plantations.[8] The Portuguese also brought laborers to these islands from Europe, including indentured servants, condemned prisoners, and orphans, but they relied increasingly on African slaves by the end of the sixteenth century.

As the European taste for sugar increased, sugar cultivation spread and influenced the growing demand for slaves. According to historian Stuart Schwartz,

> Sugar was a distinctive crop: it called not only for good land and a particular climate but also for particularly heavy capital investment in buildings and equipment and a large labor force dedicated to continual and heavy activity during certain periods of the year . . . Europeans engaged in few activities more complex than sugar production in the early modern period.[9]

Forced labor became a necessity because the intense regimen required for harvesting sugarcane and toiling at the sugar mills had no appeal to workers who had a choice.

Dawn of the Transatlantic Slave Trade

When the Portuguese explored the African coast during the fifteenth century, they frequently captured Africans. Ten Africans were taken from the Mauritanian coast in 1441, and 240 were shipped to Lisbon three years later. As the Portuguese moved farther south to more populated areas, they discovered that Africans skillfully maneuvered their coastal vessels and defended themselves well against slave raids. Subsequently, the Portuguese decided to negotiate peace treaties with African rulers and trade with them. This became the standard practice, and most slaves were purchased from African merchants and shipped to European markets.[10]

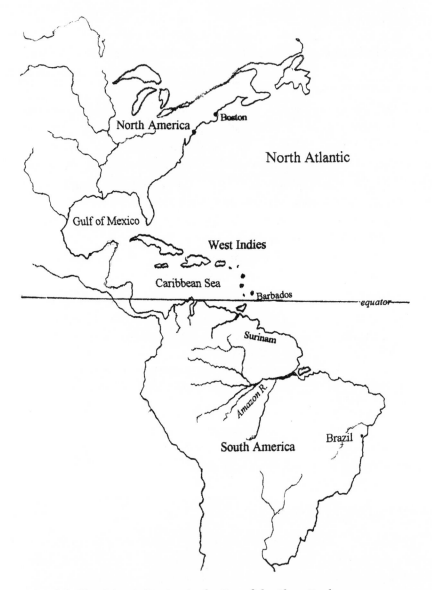

Map 1.1 The Atlantic Region in the Era of the Slave Trade

During the sixteenth century, an estimated fifty thousand African slaves were shipped to Europe, many of whom were transshipped to the Atlantic islands and later to the American colonies. After the Portuguese established sugar plantations on the African islands of São Tomé and Príncipe at the end of the fifteenth century, they transported

Map 1.1 The Atlantic Region in the Era of the Slave Trade (*Continued*)

slave labor directly from the nearby African mainland. African slaves soon outnumbered forced labor from Europe. By 1650, an estimated twenty-five thousand enslaved Africans had been taken to the North Atlantic islands and nearly one hundred thousand to Sâo Tomé (see map 1.1).[11]

By 1500, the Portuguese had explored the entire western coast of Africa, established commercial relations with African merchants, and, with the approval of African leaders, set up several coastal trading stations. In 1482, they built a fortified trading castle, São Jorga d'Elmina, which served as their headquarters on the West African coast for 155 years (see illustration 4). Until 1637, the Portuguese enjoyed a virtual trading monopoly in the region, breached only by occasional interlopers from other European nations. One of these was the English privateer John Hawkins, who embarked on three slaving expeditions during the 1560s and kidnapped several African villagers.[12]

The Slave Trade and American Colonization

The Portuguese monopoly of African trade was based on the 1494 Treaty of Tordesillas, which divided the world between Spain and Portugal, then the two dominant maritime empires. The treaty gave the Western Hemisphere to Spain, and Africa and Asia to Portugal. The consequences of this treaty were far reaching. Spain developed an empire in the Americas, except for Brazil, which was east of the Tordesillas line, but was denied direct access to Africa. When the Spanish king Philip II also became king of Portugal in 1580, the Portuguese supplied African slaves to the Spanish colonies, but when the Royal Union ended in 1640, Spain had to rely on other European carriers.

Initially, the Spanish used various methods to force Amerindians to work in mines and in agriculture, and they enslaved prisoners of war.[13] But catastrophic diseases such as measles and smallpox, carried across the Atlantic from the Old World, reduced the indigenous American population to a fraction of what it had been before Columbus arrived. This tremendous loss of life convinced some Europeans to protect the Amerindians and find other laborers. Spanish mistreatment of Amerindians prompted the Catholic priest Bartolomé de Las Casas to suggest that Africans were more suitable workers than the native population, and to his later regret, he urged the increase of African slave importation.[14] The Portuguese raided Amerindian communities and enslaved their inhabitants. The Jesuit priest Fernâo Cardim interceded on their behalf and persuaded the Portuguese king to outlaw Amerindian slavery in Brazil in 1570.[15]

Africans accompanied the earliest European explorers and settlers to America. Some may have been free, and others were treated as indentured servants and gained their freedom after a number of years. The first known African slaves brought to America were taken to Hispaniola (Haiti and the Dominican Republic) in 1502. The first transports were relatively small and came from Europe, including a group of some 250 African slaves who were shipped from Lisbon to the New World in 1510. Eight years later, Spanish American colonists requested that slaves be shipped directly from Africa. Spanish officials favored this alternative because they did not want enslaved Moors (former rulers of the Iberian Peninsula) to gain influence in the colonies. Spanish government officials also saw financial benefits in this direct African American traffic. In 1513, they introduced a system of licenses that entitled merchants to ship slaves to the colonies. This practice was modified in 1595, creating the so-called *asiento* system, which regulated the importation of slaves to the colonies through the sale of government contracts.[16]

The *asiento* managers sold subcontracts to various shipping firms to transport several thousand slaves per year to Spanish America (as document 8 illustrates). Initially, the Spanish relied completely on Portuguese shippers to deliver slaves, but when the two countries became enemies in 1640, Spain had to turn to merchant companies like the Dutch West India Company (1664–92), then briefly to French, and finally to British companies (1713–50). It was not until the nineteenth century that Spain gained a foothold in Africa and could use its own firms to obtain slaves.

The Portuguese colony in Brazil developed later than its Spanish counterparts, but eventually became the largest market for slaves. The Portuguese tried to enslave Amerindians, but this method failed to meet their labor needs. As sugar cultivation expanded during the second half of the sixteenth century, the demand for African labor increased. The first African slaves appear to have been shipped to Brazil in 1538, and this importation was legalized in 1549. The first direct shipment from Africa arrived in 1550, but it was not until about 1600 that Black slaves became the primary workforce on Brazilian plantations.[17] Thereafter, slave imports to Brazil grew steadily. During the 1690s, the newly discovered gold mines at Minas Gerais in central Brazil required large numbers of slaves, and the introduction of coffee plantations in southern Brazil demanded increased slave labor during the early nineteenth century. When the Atlantic slave trade ended in the mid–nineteenth century, Brazil had imported more than 40 percent of all slaves shipped across the Atlantic.

Why Slaves from Africa?

Why did Europeans go to Africa to get workers for the development of their American colonies? It has been argued that it would have been cheaper to enslave Europeans and ship them to the colonies. Initially, Europeans did ship their own convicts, prisoners of war, orphans, and indentured servants to the American colonies. Before 1640, there were still more European and Amerindian bonded laborers in the Caribbean than people of African descent. Ultimately, however, Africans became the preferred labor force, partially because of European culture and values. Although Europeans often exploited their workers harshly, treated their social inferiors with disdain, and punished offenders brutally, including torture and cruel executions, they increasingly refrained from reducing them to slavery. Only outsiders, people who were different and had no roots in a community, were made chattel slaves.[18] In that sense, Europeans acted like Muslims, who enslaved outsiders or "infidels" but protected fellow Muslims from that fate.

Also, Europeans went to Africa to get slaves because they could buy them there at a reasonable price. As long as slaves could be purchased in Africa, which was virtually between Europe and America, the traffic could be expanded into a lucrative triangular commerce.

In the early years of the traffic, Europeans sometimes kidnapped Africans. This became a rarity, however, as the slave trade became a regular business in which African and European merchants cooperated to their mutual advantage and at the expense of the unfortunate victims. Africa's enormous diversity in culture and states also favored European interests. A thousand different languages and ethnic groups and numerous states existed side by side in Africa. The more powerful states could easily exploit the weaker ones while protecting their own subjects. A few coastal states, such as early Benin in today's Nigeria, refused to sell people, but the lure of profits and imported foreign goods tempted many rulers and merchants. Thus, European merchants could buy slaves at various trading posts along the coast.

As slavery spread across the Atlantic, it gradually transformed into an institution linked to a single racial group, Black Africans, and from which escape was virtually impossible. Most Africans could readily be distinguished from Europeans; they looked different, spoke very different languages, had different customs, and were rarely Christians at the time of their enslavement. Ethnic differences were always important distinctions between human communities, but they could fade over time. Racial features, on the other hand, passed from one generation to another and were impossible to hide. In time, African or Black became synonymous with slave, and racism became a sinister new element of American slavery, one that has haunted America to this day.

How and Why Africans Were Enslaved

Before the nineteenth century, Europeans lacked the ability to penetrate the interior of Africa. The limited range of the guns from their ships, fortified coastal castles, and their susceptibility to tropical diseases prevented all but a few Europeans from venturing inland. Because half of the Europeans stationed on the Guinea Coast died during their first year, this region became known as "the white man's grave."[19] Europe's primitive firearm technology, incapable of overpowering most African states during the slave trade era, made cooperative treaties between Europeans and Africans essential for commercial activities. Only after the development of automatic rifles and the discovery that linked germs with diseases were Europeans able to conquer Africa, albeit with stiff resistance from many African states.[20] By that time, however, the Atlantic slave trade had ended.

As in other parts of the world, Africans were enslaved through warfare, indebtedness, or judicial process. Some were enslaved to settle conflicts between rival communities or serve as tribute to a political overlord. Drought and famine drove others into slavery, especially children whose parents were unable to feed them. As demand for slaves in the New World escalated, some African leaders resorted to slave raids.[21] Olaudah Equiano and his sister were probably captured in such a raid (as is depicted in document 1).

Initially, Europeans were more interested in African gold and ivory than in slaves. However, as demand for labor in the Americas increased and Africans became enamored of imported luxury goods, African merchants were willing to trade slaves for Asian textiles, European tools and firearms, and American tobacco and alcoholic beverages.

Slaves and Tropical Produce

Europeans also developed a taste for luxury imports, primarily sugar and coffee, grown at tropical plantations with African slave labor. The spread of sugar cultivation in the 1600s stimulated the expansion of the Atlantic slave trade dramatically. After sugar production became successful in Brazil, the Dutch sought to dominate the industry by capturing northern Brazil in 1630, which got them started in the traffic. Although the Portuguese regained all of Brazil a few decades later, the Dutch remained active in the slave trade. Some of the planters who had cooperated with the Dutch fled Brazil and settled in the Caribbean, where they helped to establish sugarcane cultivation. This expansion of sugar agriculture has sometimes been referred to as the "sugar revolution."[22]

The English established sugar plantations in the Caribbean, most prominently in Barbados and Jamaica, and the French developed St. Domingue (Haiti), Martinique, and Guadeloupe as sugar-producing islands. Other commodities desired by Europeans, such as coffee, tobacco, indigo, and later cotton, were also grown at plantation colonies. Slave labor was the most convenient system for plantations, and the flow of slaves from Africa changed from a trickle to a flood in the mid–seventeenth century. David Eltis explains the rapid increase of the slave trade at that time:

> The numbers of enslaved Africans crossing the Atlantic before the north-western Europeans took up the business were modest compared to what came later. It was only after 1650 that the slave systems of the Americas expanded drastically and intensified in the sense that the basis of slavery was now the plantation complex, not the highly varied types of slave employment to be found in the early Spanish Americas.[23]

In Barbados, for example, bonded European laborers predominated until 1660, after which the labor force primarily shifted to African slaves. The Dutch established thriving plantation colonies on the Guiana coast at the Surinam and Essequibo Rivers, and the French at Cayenne.

North American mainland colonies were relatively late in import-
ing African slaves, as plantations were not widespread in the English
and Dutch settlements along the eastern coast. The first African slaves
in what later became the United States were probably brought to
Florida by the Spanish. Better remembered, however, are the slaves who
landed at Jamestown, Virginia, in 1619, as recorded by Virginia chroni-
cler John Smith: "About the last of August came a Dutch man-of-warre
that sold us twenty negars."[24]

Although enslaved Africans could be found throughout the Americas, it was not until the eighteenth century that they were brought in
large numbers to the southern mainland colonies, to work on plantations growing tobacco, indigo, rice, and cotton. Still, compared with
Brazil and the Caribbean region, the number of enslaved Africans
brought to the North American mainland was relatively small.

Slave Trade Regions in Africa

Slaves were obtained at many African coastal regions, but three
general areas dominated the trade. The largest was the Guinea Coast,
which exported more than half of the slaves crossing the Atlantic. This
area was subdivided into smaller regions, some of which Europeans
identified by their exports. Starting from the west, the first area was
named for its rivers Senegal and Gambia, also known as Senegambia.
Next came the Grain Coast or Upper Guinea, consisting of today's
Guinea, Sierra Leone, and Liberia, followed by the Ivory Coast, the
Gold Coast, and the Slave Coast. Further east was the delta of the Niger
River, and finally the Cameroons. The second general area involved in
the slave trade, both in size and numbers of slaves exported, was west-
central Africa. Usually called Angola by contemporaries, it included
today's Angola as well as the area north of the Congo River to the
Cameroons. Least important of the three general areas was the southeast coast of Africa, which produced about 4.5 percent of the slaves who
crossed the Atlantic.

Institutions and Methods of Slaving

The Atlantic slave trade was a cooperative venture between European and African merchants and their respective rulers. With few excep-

tions, Africans were responsible for enslavement and transportation to coastal outlets. Europeans provided the ships, the capital, and the commercial organization to transport the slaves across the Atlantic and sell them at American destinations. Because these human cargoes represented large investments and were always at great risk of suffering losses, transporting them was a complicated and precarious enterprise. Ship crews were often twice as large as those of ordinary cargo ships because slaves were unwilling passengers, likely to resist, and might even jump overboard. During the early stages of European expansion, governments often lacked the financial resources for overseas ventures and relied on merchants to take the initiative. With government encouragement and support, merchants pooled their resources and created joint-stock companies, which played crucial roles as precursors for colonial expansion. Prominent among these enterprises were the English Royal African Company, the Dutch West India Company, and the French Guinea Company. Authorized by government charters, they received special monopoly rights over commerce in their respective regions and were responsible for maintaining trading stations. Although these companies traded a variety of goods, the slave trade often figured prominently in their activities.

The chartered companies stationed agents at trading factories to exchange a variety of merchandise with African traders. The African merchandise, including slaves, was temporarily kept at the trading stations until a company ship arrived from Europe. This "fixed location" method, also known as castle trade, permitted ships to load cargoes quickly and shortened coastal stays.

Toward the end of the seventeenth century, private merchants who demanded that trade remain free and open to all merchants in the country challenged the monopolies of the charter companies. Both France and England reduced or abandoned monopolies and allowed private merchants to participate in the African trade after paying a specified fee. The English "ten-percenters," named for the fee or tax they paid, became prominent participants in the slave trade after 1698.

The shift toward free trade changed the way slaves were obtained. No longer able to get the same services at company-run trading stations, ships often sailed along the coast in search of African merchants with slaves to sell. Some captains sent a boat, often referred to as the "long boat," upriver or along the coast to contact African merchants (see document 6). This mobile method of trading was usually referred to as "coasting." Because it often took longer to accumulate a full cargo under this system, slaves purchased early had to spend more time aboard ship. Free traders tried to offset this limitation by using smaller and faster ships.

European-based slave ships followed a transatlantic pattern that has often been described as triangular, carrying merchandise from Europe to Africa, transporting slaves from there to the Americas, and returning to Europe with American-grown commodities. However, when the slave trade reached a peak during the eighteenth century, the return voyage to Europe was often completed with just a token cargo or none at all (in ballast). It was inefficient for slave ships to wait for a full cargo when the demand for slaves was strong; they had to prepare for the next slave voyage, and it was often cheaper to ship American-grown commodities to Europe in regular cargo ships with smaller crews. Slave traders based in Brazil followed a bilateral pattern, directly between Brazil and Africa. North American–based slave ships often operated a small triangular trade by selling their slaves in the West Indies and shipping molasses and rum back to New England.

International Rivalry and Wars

European trading stations in Africa were often fortified with cannons pointing seaward to defend against European rivals. These stations were invariably established with local African approval and were rarely attacked by Africans. Trading stations could be found in many coastal regions, but some African rulers did not permit them. Europeans were usually prevented from building forts in the Niger Delta region and in the region north of the Congo River. Generally, European control did not extend into the interior until the nineteenth-century era of colonialism. The exception was Angola, where the Portuguese exerted considerable influence in the interior through cooperation with local rulers and with assistance from racially mixed offspring of Portuguese and Africans, called Luso-Africans.[25]

On the Slave Coast, some rulers insisted that competing European nations have equal access to their markets. Others favored specific nationalities and prevented their rivals from doing business in the area. This happened during the 1730s, when King Agaja ousted the Dutch from the expanding Dahomey State on the Slave Coast and allowed the Portuguese to build a fortified trading station.

Because European states were generally commercial rivals, their colonial interests occasionally led to war. Such wars impacted their commercial interests in various ways. They conquered each other's colonies and trading stations, captured each other's ships, practiced legalized piracy through privateering, and sought alliances with friendly European and African states to gain advantages.

Wars between traditional rivals France and Britain generally favored the rising British Empire, with its powerful navy. When the French were cut off from their colonies, they often had to rely on neutral nations to supply slaves and provisions. Widespread European warfare disrupted Atlantic commerce in 1690–1715 and again in 1740–63. French and Dutch support for the Americans during their Revolutionary War (1775–83) virtually halted the slave trade of these two countries. The French Revolutionary Wars (1792–1815) did not interrupt the slave trade but changed the relative commercial balance among nations, increasing the power of Britain in the long run.

Wars in Africa also impacted the slave trade. While they increased the availability of slaves by producing prisoners, they also often closed the trade routes, making it difficult for merchants to move goods to coastal outlets. Many of these wars were small in scale and limited to a specific region, but the rising new states of Asante (Gold Coast) and Dahomey (Slave Coast) expanded to the coast during the early eighteenth century, interrupting existing commercial contacts. The decline of the state of Oyo in central Nigeria during the early nineteenth century resulted in the enslavement of many of its subjects, many of whom were transported across the Atlantic. The Angola hinterland in west-central Africa was plagued by incessant political instability from the sixteenth to the nineteenth centuries, and the demand for slaves and slave raids were a drain on the region's population.[26]

Despite these disruptions, the numbers of slaves transported to the Americas peaked in the period from 1726 to 1850. More than 75 percent of all the slaves involved in the Atlantic slave trade were shipped across the ocean during those 125 years.

Ending Slavery and the Slave Trade

The termination of the Atlantic slave trade was a complex process that took nearly a century to be completed. Starting with a few isolated critics, an abolitionist movement grew that changed public opinion and influenced the British and U.S. governments to declare the slave trade illegal by 1808. Diplomatic pressure gradually forced other countries to do the same by the 1850s. Because the traffic continued illegally, various programs were established to suppress it.

The largest forced migration in human history ended when the last slave ship sailed across the Atlantic in 1867. It was not until 1888, however, that Brazil became the last country in the Western Hemisphere to abolish slavery. The labor systems that replaced slavery were often far from free.[27] Slavery persisted in other parts of the world well into the twentieth century, and reports of slavery in the form of sexual and labor exploitation persist to this day.

Although a 1926 conference in Geneva, Switzerland, aimed at abolishing slavery worldwide signed the Convention to Suppress the Slave Trade and Slavery, its goals were not realized. In 1953, a special United Nations conference approved a new covenant to "intensify national as well as international efforts toward the abolition of slavery, the slave trade and practices similar to slavery."[28]

Notes

1. Orlando Patterson, *Slavery and Social Death: A Comparative Study* (Cambridge, Mass.: Harvard University Press, 1982), vii.

2. David Brion Davis, *The Problem of Slavery in Western Culture* (Ithaca, N.Y.: Cornell University Press, 1966), 35–36, 43.

3. Paul Lovejoy, *Transformations of Slavery: A History of Slavery in Africa*, 2d ed. (New York: Cambridge University Press, 2000), 1.

4. See Suzanne Miers and Igor Kopytoff, eds., *Slavery in Africa* (Madison: University of Wisconsin Press, 1977).

5. Stephen Clissold, *The Barbary Slaves* (1977; reprint, New York: Barnes & Noble, 1992).

6. Davis, *Problem of Slavery,* 41–46; Philip D. Curtin, "Slavery and Empire," in *Comparative Perspectives on Slavery in New World Plantation Societies,* ed. Vera Rubin and Arthur Tuden (New York: Academy of Sciences, 1977), 9–10.

7. Ralph A. Austin, "The Trans-Saharan Slave Trade: A Tentative Census," in *The Uncommon Market,* ed. Henry A. Gemery and Jan S. Hogendorn (New York: Academic Press, 1979), 23–76.

8. William D. Phillips, Jr., *Slavery from Roman Times to the Early Transatlantic Trade* (Minneapolis: University of Minnesota Press, 1985), 168–69.

9. Stuart B. Schwartz, *Slaves, Peasants, and Rebels: Reconsidering Brazilian Slavery* (Urbana: University of Illinois Press, 1996), 40.

10. John Thornton, *Africa and Africans in the Making of the Atlantic World, 1400–1800*, 2d ed. (New York: Cambridge University Press, 1998), 30–36.

11. Phillips, *Slavery from Roman Times*, 193; Philip D. Curtin, *The Atlantic Slave Trade: A Census* (Madison: University of Wisconsin Press, 1969), 20.

12. Clements R. Markham, "The Hawkins' Voyages during the Reigns of Henry VIII, Queen Elizabeth, and James I," in *The Hakluyt Society*, First Series (1878; reprint, New York: Burt Franklin Publisher, 1970), 20–24, 70–72.

13. Phillips, *Slavery from Roman Times*, 174.

14. See introduction by Bill M. Donovan in Bartolomé de Las Casas, *The Devastation of the Indies: A Brief Account* (1552, first Spanish edition; Baltimore, Md.: Johns Hopkins University Press, 1992).

15. Charles R. Boxer, *The Portuguese Seaborne Empire, 1415–1825* (New York: Knopf, 1969), 91–94; Phillips, *Slavery from Roman Times*, 180. See also Alfred C. Crosby, Jr., *The Columbian Exchange: Biological and Cultural Consequences of 1492* (Westport, Conn.: Greenwood Press, 1972), 35–63.

16. Georges Scelle, "The Slave Trade in the Spanish Colonies of America: The Asiento," *American Journal of International Law* 4 (1910): 612–61.

17. Phillips, *Slavery from Roman Times*, 182, 191; Collin A. Palmer, *The First Passage: Blacks in the Americas, 1502–1617* (Oxford: Oxford University Press, 1995), 55.

18. See David Eltis, *The Rise of African Slavery in the Americas* (New York: Cambridge University Press, 2000), chapter 3.

19. Kenneth F. Kiple and Virginia Himmelsteib King, *Another Dimension to the Black Diaspora: Diet, Disease, and Racism* (New York: Cambridge University Press, 1981), 12.

20. See Daniel R. Headrick, *The Tools of Empire* (Oxford: Oxford University Press, 1981).

21. For the process of enslavement, see Thornton, *Africa and Africans in the Making of the Atlantic World*, 98–125.

22. Elisabeth Donnan, *Documents Illustrative of the Slave Trade to America*, 4 vols. (Washington, D.C.: Carnegie Institution, 1931), 1:125 and 135.

23. David Eltis, *The Rise of African Slavery in the Americas*, 27, 41.

24. Vincent Harlow, ed., *Colonizing Expeditions to the West Indies and Guiana, 1623–1667*, Hakluyt Society, Series 2 (London: Hakluyt Society, 1925), 56:25.

25. Joseph C. Miller, *Way of Death: Merchant Capitalism and the Angolan Slave Trade, 1730–1830* (Madison: University of Wisconsin Press, 1988), 245–83.

26. See Miller, *Way of Death*, chapter 4.

27. See Michael Twaddle, *The Wages of Slavery: From Chattel Slavery to Wage Labour in Africa, The Caribbean and England* (London: Frank Cass, 1993).

28. The Avalon Project of the Yale Law School, "Supplementary Convention on the Abolition of Slavery, the Slave Trade . . . " *http://www.yale.edu/lawweb/avalon/un/slave56.htm*.

CHAPTER 2

DREADFUL JOURNEYS TO A NEW WORLD

A Chain of Suffering and Death

The crossing of the Atlantic Ocean from the African coast to American shores is known as the Middle Passage. It was only one part of the long passage between initial enslavement and final destination, but for many students of the slave trade it has come to symbolize the entire journey. Although usually shorter than other legs of the long trek, for the slaves it was a horrible experience and a dramatic break with the past. William Wilberforce (1759–1833), a leading British abolitionist, once said: "Never can so much misery be found condensed in so small a place as in a slave ship during the Middle Passage."[1] The few enslaved Africans who were able to leave accounts of their experiences portray it as a dreadful experience, and many crew members and other witnesses confirm the unbearable conditions aboard slave ships.

The slaves' journey from their home in Africa to the New World invariably included capture and enslavement in Africa, the trek to the coast where they were sold and detained, boarding and coast-time on the slave ship, the ocean crossing or Middle Passage, disembarkation and sale in the Americas, and then inland travel or a secondary voyage. This trip was followed by a period of adjustment to a new environment—the "seasoning" process, as Caribbean planters sometimes called it.

Enslavement and March to the Coast

A person could be enslaved through various means, including imprisonment in war or capture during a slave raid. Persons born into slavery in Africa were considered domestic slaves, who were rarely sold and were as a rule gradually integrated into their communities. Slaves placed in the commercial network, many of whom ended up in the Atlantic system, were known as trade slaves. Domestic slaves could become trade slaves because of disobedience or criminal behavior, or to settle disputes or serve as tribute payment to an overlord. As the demand for slaves in the Americas increased, larger numbers of domestic slaves were sold into the commercial network.

Very little firsthand information survives about the enslavement process and the march to the coast. The memoir accounts of Equiano and Ayuba (presented in documents 1 and 4) are rare exceptions, and neither may have been a typical experience. In most cases, the journey to the coast involved weeks, if not months, of walking, under brutal conditions and a cloud of uncertainty. Slaves were usually tied together in column-caravans, also known as coffles, as the European explorer Mungo Park (1771–1806) describes in document 2 (see illustration 1). Often they were used as beasts of burden, forced to carry merchandise for their temporary owners. Periodic and nightly halts were made along the road or at trading stations, where some slaves were sold to other slave merchants or local residents. In this way, some escaped the ocean voyage and, although still enslaved, remained in more familiar African surroundings. Because few if any records of these overland journeys exist, we can only speculate about the experiences of the victims. In his book *Way of Death,* Joseph Miller tried to capture the agony and dangers that slaves experienced on marches in Angola:

> Exposure to the dry-season chill in the high elevations and to damp nights spent sitting in open pathside camps, utter lack of clothing and shelter . . . contributed to the appearance of respiratory ailments . . . [Slaves] grew weaker and more susceptible to parasites and other diseases that swept in epidemic form through the coffles. The slave trade must have been a veritable incubator for typhus, typhoid, and other fevers. . . . The . . . lethal consequences of malnutrition, disease, and other hardships along the path were death rates that rose at an increasing tempo . . . perhaps to catastrophic levels in the range of 400–600 per 1,000 per annum by the time slaves reached the coast.[2]

A nineteenth-century abolitionist, Thomas Fowell Buxton (1786–1845), estimated that more than half of the enslaved died in

Africa before reaching the European slave ships. A recent study about the Angola slave trade also estimates high pre-embarkation losses of approximately 25 percent from death and flight, and another 15 percent during coastal detainment.[3] Some of the personal narratives of slaves, however, mention high mortality in the enslavement process, but not on their march to the coast. For example, Equiano's seven-month trek to the Guinea Coast depicts a fairly orderly journey, with several lengthy delays, but does not mention high death rates along the way (see document 1). The experience varied from one place and time to another, and while many slaves must have died before the Middle Passage started, mortality figures in Africa remain a matter of speculation.

Coastal Trauma

Arriving at the African coast must have been a shock for most of the slaves. Were they awestruck by the huge body of water and the oceangoing ships anchored off the coast? Were they overcome by apprehension of what awaited them, crossing this large body of water from which return seemed impossible? This was the first time many encountered Europeans, with their light skin, bearded faces, and strange-sounding speech. Arrival at the coast brought a crucial transfer of ownership to Europeans, who subjected slaves to humiliating physical examinations (illustrated in document 5). After the sale price was negotiated, slaves were usually branded with a red-hot iron, which marked them with a number or symbol indicating their new owners (see illustration 2).

As people from various locations merged on the African coast, germs carried by Europeans from across the ocean and by slaves from the African interior threatened everyone—slaves and traders alike—with illness and death. Some diseases did not manifest themselves until the ocean crossing or after arrival in the Americas.

While waiting for a ship, slaves were often detained in warehouse space or in castle dungeons, like the one at the Cape Coast castle at Accra, Ghana, which can still be visited today. Where no buildings were available, as was often the case on the Slave Coast and at Angola, slaves were kept in open pens or stockades on or near the beach. Miller's description of the stockades (barracoons) in Benguela, Angola, tries to capture the appalling conditions:

> The great majority of the slaves went directly to the slave pens . . .
> living for days and weeks surrounded by walls too high for a per-
> son to scale, squatting helplessly, naked, on the dirt and entirely
> exposed to the skies except for a few adjoining cells where they
> could be locked at night. They lived in a 'wormy morass' and slept
> in their own excrement. . . . To the smell of rotting fish were added
> the foul odors of the slaves' dysentery and the putrid fragrance of
> the bodies of those who died. . . . [T]raders simply threw out the
> bodies of the slaves on the beach along with sewage until the very
> end of the eighteenth century.[4]

During this wait, slaves were sometimes put to work at trading stations.
If a ship was already anchored off the coast, however, they were quickly
ferried to it. Going through the heavy surf in coastal rowboats and
being hoisted aboard the ship was no doubt a frightening introduction
to the Atlantic Ocean. Some slaves drowned in the boarding process,
either accidentally or while trying to escape. Once onboard, they were
generally confined between decks, where they waited until the ship had
boarded enough slaves to start the Middle Passage. Sometimes this
coasting period lasted many months (see illustration 3).

    Rumors frequently spread among the slaves that the strange White
men were cannibals who planned to eat them or take them to a faraway
land to be eaten. The big kettles in which their food was cooked might
have reinforced the fear, and an improved diet at this stage might also
have fueled such rumors, although this was actually intended to assure
their survival and a profitable resale at American markets.

The Middle Passage

    Ships used for the slave trade were regular freight vessels inter-
nally restructured to carry human cargoes. They varied in size and carrying capacity, the majority about 50–125 feet long and 8–15 feet wide,
averaging 100 to 300 ton. The larger ones transported five hundred
or more slaves, and the smaller ones fewer than one hundred. By
mid–nineteenth century, a few very large ships carried more than one
thousand slaves each, but this was during the final years of the illicit
slave trade. Regardless of size, the space allowed for slaves was much
less than that provided to emigrants and soldiers going from Europe to
the colonies.[5]

Slave ships carried merchandise on their first leg from Europe to Africa, and from America to Europe they often carried American commodities. As slave vessels initially approached their African destinations, some cargo was brought on deck so the ship's carpenters could remodel the interior, installing platforms between decks on which slaves would spend most of their time. Bulkheads, or partitions, separated the sexes and age groups and retarded the spread of slave insurrections.

Although conditions aboard slave ships varied, most Europeans used similar methods for transporting slaves, as historian Herbert Klein explains:

> By the middle decades of the 18th century . . . all Europeans carried approximately the same number of slaves in the same types of ships, and crossed the Atlantic in the same amount of time. They also housed and fed their slave passengers in approximately the same way. Thus the many European slave trades can be considered as one general European slave trade.[6]

Most slaves were crammed into their designated spaces like loaves of bread on a shelf, with an average of six to seven square feet and rarely more than two or three feet of head space. Abolitionists tried to illustrate the dreadfully crowded conditions aboard slave ships with drawings of the ship *Brookes,* which got the point across without being fully realistic. A more realistic illustration is that of the interior space on the French slave ship *L'Aurore,* which leaves spaces to reach the slaves (see illustrations 5 and 6).

Men slaves were generally shackled two by two, making movement extremely difficult, and small groups were strung together by a longer chain to take them to the upper deck for meals and fresh air. Women and children were generally confined to a separate deck space or in cabins and allowed greater mobility. Because men were stronger and nearly always in the majority, they were securely confined to prevent the possibility of rebellion. Sick slaves were sometimes released from their chains, and women were often employed in the preparation of food. Some slave ships, particularly those with large transports, often had a few slaves working as translators or healers, while others helped with various onboard chores.

Slaves were periodically taken on deck in groups to eat and to get fresh air. Most slave ships had drums onboard to encourage slaves to dance and get some exercise. Slave quarters were periodically cleaned during these breaks, although weather and shortage of personnel might interfere with these hygienic measures. In any case, the stench below decks was usually unbearable, as Equiano has so vividly described in document 6.

As a rule, slaves were given two or three meals a day, but the number of meals depended on the availability of food and weather conditions. Beans and other staples brought from Europe were cooked in large iron pots on deck. African staples, such as rice, maize, yams, and meat from small livestock, added some variety to the otherwise bland soup or mush. While still on the African coast and before the full complement of slaves was boarded, food supplies were ample, but if the Middle Passage lasted longer than expected, rations were reduced. Insufficient and spoiled drinking water was often a serious problem.

The swaying of the ship must have caused seasickness among the slaves, who came predominantly from the African interior. Buckets in which slaves could relieve themselves were apparently available at a few locations, but the chains must have made them difficult to reach when needed. Some slaves had to lie in their own and each other's excrement, a condition that one author called "more easily imagined than described."[7] Illness spread easily, especially the common afflictions of diarrhea and the so-called red flux, when blood was in the stools.

Illness and Death on the Middle Passage

Although European owners and transporters of slaves wanted as many as possible to arrive in good condition and produce a profit for them, malnutrition prior to boarding and deprivation of sunlight from prolonged stays below deck made illness and high death rates unavoidable.[8]

Ships carrying large numbers of slaves usually had at least one medical doctor and one or more barber-surgeons to care for sick slaves and crew members. During the eighteenth century, a growing understanding of the merits of cleanliness and fresh air, along with improvements in nutrition and medical treatment, undoubtedly contributed to the decline in mortality rates. On the whole, however, medical science during the age of the slave trade was still quite primitive, and attempts at curing illness may have done more harm than good. The presence of barber-surgeons indicates that bleeding was still used, a practice that robbed patients of the remedial merits of blood and often shortened lives rather than prolonging them. Modern medicine, based on the germ theory of disease, did not become prevalent until the end of the nineteenth century, after the Atlantic slave trade was abolished.

Many doctors kept records of the treatment administered to slaves, and most maintained death lists, registering the dates and causes of slave deaths. According to these records, approximately two-thirds of the deaths were caused by malaria, yellow fever, and intestinal disorders. The remainder resulted from smallpox, scurvy, slave revolts, suicides, and other causes.[9]

Duration and Patterns of Slave Voyages

Compared with modern ships powered by steam or diesel-fueled engines, sail-powered ships used in the slave trade were slow. Sometimes they had to wait several weeks before suitable wind conditions allowed them to leave their European ports. Voyages from Europe to Africa lasted two to three months, depending on weather, port of origin, and destination. The time that slave ships remained on the African coast varied greatly, rarely less than one month and sometimes half a year or longer. The Middle Passage usually lasted fifty to eighty days, depending on point of departure and American destination, although a few ships accomplished it within a month, while others took six months or more. Historian Philip Curtin describes some of the complications involved in the ocean crossing:

> A ship from Senegambia could move directly into the northeast trade winds for a relatively short and predictable passage to the Caribbean. The Guinea Coast, however, had prevailing westerly winds and a strong current flowing towards the east. The usual voyage, and the route still recommended for sailing ships bound from the Guinea Coast to the North Atlantic, took the ship south to the equator to pick up the southeast trades. Then in mid-ocean, it turned northward across the equatorial calms to catch the northeast trades for the Caribbean. Thus, a ship bound for the northern hemisphere had to cross the doldrums [windless periods] twice with slaves on board, each time taking a chance on prolonged calms which could mean shortages of food and water and a greater danger of disease in the crowded slave quarters.[10]

With favorable winds, the ocean crossing could be completed in a matter of weeks, but that was exceptionally swift. The Cambridge University Press Database demonstrates that fewer than 8 percent of the slave ships managed to complete the Middle Passage in less than one month, while 77 percent made it across the Atlantic in less than eighty days, and 23 percent required more than eighty days.[11] Duration of the voyage affected the suffering of the slaves as well as the potential profits of the slave traders.

Hazards along the Way

The Middle Passage posed a variety of dangers that could harm and kill many slaves. In addition to illness, slaves might face serious shortages of food and water if voyages lasted longer than planned. They might also have to endure dangerous storms, the doldrums, and attacks by pirates, privateers, and other enemies.

One of the most tragic storm-related catastrophes occurred in 1738 on the Dutch slave ship *Leusden*. The ship left Elmina in West Africa with a transport of 716 slaves on November 19, 1737, and had an unusually quick voyage. On January 1, 1738, however, just a few days before reaching its destination port in Surinam, the ship was caught in a vicious storm that stranded it on rocks near the river Marawin. According to the reports of surviving officers, as the storm raged, the ship began to tilt to one side and take on water, making rescue of the human cargo impossible. In order to avoid a scramble for the lifeboats, the crew closed the hatches and locked the slaves below decks, where they all drowned or suffocated before the storm ended a few days later.

Of the 716 slaves boarded in Africa, only fourteen, who were doing chores on deck when the storm began, survived. There is no record of how many slaves died before the storm, but because of the relatively quick crossing, the mortality rate may have been less than 5 percent. Thus, approximately 665 slaves died as a result of the shipwreck. This may well have been the worst catastrophe of its kind in the Atlantic slave trade. The seventy-three surviving crew members and fourteen slaves managed to reach Paramaribo in the lifeboats on January 4, where the slaves were subsequently sold. Because of the enormous financial loss, West India Company directors were keenly interested in the disaster and ordered all officers of the ship to make depositions. The officers claimed that if they had released the slaves, a fight over the few lifeboats would most likely have killed everyone. It is perhaps no coincidence that soon after this tragedy, the company stopped transporting slaves across the Atlantic.[12]

The heavy rains, common during the wet season in tropical regions, also affected the experience aboard slave ships. They often prevented slaves from going on deck to catch fresh air, made the foul air below decks worse, and accelerated the spread of disease. Another weather-related problem was the lack of wind, the equatorial calms or doldrums, that rendered sail-driven ships helpless and often lengthened voyages considerably.

Slave ships also ran the danger of being captured by pirates, privateers, or other hostile ships in wartime. While a shift from one European owner to another might in itself have made little difference to the slaves, the process may have endangered their lives and made the Middle Passage longer. A battle at sea could kill slaves as innocent bystanders or sink the ship with slaves shackled below decks. Most European ships carried protective papers, so-called Turkish passes, as a safeguard against capture by pirates from North Africa. Privateers were usually a threat only in time of war, when governments authorized some of their subjects to inflict damage on enemies.

Slave Treatment and Sexual Exploitation

Conditions aboard slave ships were harsh enough, but maltreatment of slaves by crew members could make matters even worse. Captains' directives generally included instructions demanding careful treatment of slaves by the crew (illustrated in document 11). But crew members themselves were often mistreated by officers, and cruelty could readily be passed on to the slaves.

Slave trade companies usually forbade crew members to engage in sexual relations with female slaves and threatened punishment for such behavior. Still, sexual exploitation undoubtedly took place, as Captain John Newton (1725–1807) confirmed many years later (see document 7). Its prevalence, however, can only be inferred from incomplete evidence. With an all-male crew, usually quartered on the top deck, and slave women housed separately from male slaves, sexual relations between crew members and female slaves were almost certain to occur. Female slaves had no power to protect themselves against such abuse.

Slave Rebellions and Resistance

In spite of overwhelming odds, many slaves resisted their enslavement and forced exportation from Africa. Some refused to eat, while others jumped overboard when they had the chance, preferring death to the uncertainty of slavery in a strange land. Slave ship managers used force-feeding tools and outboard netting to combat such efforts and keep as many slaves alive as possible. Many slaves risked their lives in shipboard revolts, which had little chance of success and usually resulted in many deaths. The Cambridge University Press Database suggests that one in every ten slave transports experienced slave rebellion of some sort, and that as many as one hundred thousand slaves may have lost their lives in them.[13]

To prevent revolts, slave traders had to be on constant alert, especially while still on the African coast. Some observers speculated that rumors of cannibalism on the part of Whites might have driven slaves to rebel (as illustrated in document 5). Living like convicts on floating prisons with little hope for the future, slaves had many reasons to risk their lives, even though they must have realized the chances of success were slim and punishment brutal. According to British slave trade scholar David Richardson, "as far as the enslaved Africans were concerned, conditions that offered an opportunity to escape from captivity seem to have been seized on wherever and whenever they presented themselves."[14]

Although slave revolts were primarily staged by men, women may have played important roles, because they had more freedom and could get information and weapons for the men. Recent research suggests that the coastal origins of slave transports made a difference in the occurrence of shipboard rebellions. Slaves from the Upper Guinea regions were more likely to revolt than those from west central Africa and the Slave Coast. The reason for this is not completely clear, but most likely relates to their African experience and values. The occurrence of slave rebellions, as a percentage of slave transports, increased during the 1750–94 period, when the Atlantic slave trade was at its peak.[15]

It has often been suggested that slave revolts occurred more frequently in sight of the African coast, and certainly crews tended to anticipate rebellions more while near land. But rebellions also took place during the ocean crossing. The longer coasting period may have created the appearance that slaves were more prone to rebel when land was in sight. However, chances of a successful rebellion on the African coast were not much better because other European slave ships were usually nearby to offer assistance to a besieged ship. During a revolt on the Dutch slave ship *Neptunis* in 1785, slaves overpowered and killed many crew members, but a nearby British slave ship hit the powder chamber of the *Neptunis* with cannon fire and caused it to explode. Only eight slaves survived, but as they swam toward shore, they were picked up by local Africans and delivered to the captain of the ship, who happened to be ashore. Rebelling slaves on the American slave ship *Little George* in 1730 (narrated in document 10) were more successful. They reached shore at Sierra Leone and appear to have received support from the local population.

Another revolt with a very tragic outcome occurred on the ship *Middelburgs Welvaren* in 1740, when the slaves gained control of the lower but not the upper deck. The well-armed and trigger-happy crew members on the upper deck fired indiscriminately on those below, killing 213 of the 260 slaves who boarded on the Guinea coast. Thirteen slaves had died during the partial crossing, and only thirty were subsequently landed and sold in Surinam.

In 1769, another noteworthy slave revolt occurred on the ship *Guineese Vriendschap*. A Dutch warship, which happened to be in the vicinity, stopped the rebellion and restored control to the crew. Four slaves died by jumping overboard, and the alleged leader of the revolt was captured, brutally tortured, and executed as a deterrent against other uprisings. According to ship records, the rebel leader was Essjerrie Ettin (see "Biographical Sketch"), an Asante from present-day Ghana, one of the few slaves identified by name. Ringleaders of rebelling slaves aboard the French ship *Africain* met a similar fate in 1738.[16]

Occasionally, rebelling slaves managed to take control of the ship. Such seizures usually resulted in considerable loss of life among the crew, unless they were able to escape in lifeboats. The slaves who gained control of an unidentified Brazilian ship in 1812 let the captured crew take the lifeboats while they navigated the ship to an unknown destination.[17] Another successful slave revolt was the case of the *Amistad* during the 1830s, when slaves forced a few surviving crew members to navigate the ship until it eventually reached Connecticut. After a long and highly publicized court battle, the slaves gained their freedom.

The constant threat of rebellion had many consequences. It meant few mutinies on slave ships, because every crew member was needed to keep the slaves under control and crew members would rarely seek allies among the slaves. The threat of rebellion also increased the cost of the traffic, because more crew members were needed to guard the slaves. British slave trade historian David Richardson has suggested that without the threat of slave revolts the overall volume of the Atlantic slave trade might have been about 9 percent higher.[18]

Destination and Sale

Reaching land on the American side of the Atlantic must have brought a sense of relief to crew members and the enslaved passengers alike. Most destinations were in tropical or semitropical regions, and the sight of greenery must have aroused curiosity and expectation. In most instances, fresh food and water were now available, and the slaves were able to move around again, especially after they were taken ashore (see illustration 8).

In some cases, arrival brought new trials. Ships and their human cargoes were generally inspected by designated authorities. If a contagious disease such as smallpox was evident, a ship might be quarantined and entrance to the harbor postponed until the epidemic subsided. If later inspections proved that the epidemic persisted, the quarantine might continue for several weeks before disembarkation was permitted.

Once ashore, slaves were usually separated into groups based on their physical condition and appeal to buyers. The sick and infirm were often auctioned off early to avoid further losses. Prime slaves were expected to fetch the highest prices and were often sold individually or according to previously arranged contracts (as shown in document 9). Several American Atlantic ports operated slave markets, as was once common in the Mediterranean region, where slaves were sold on a regular basis (see illustration 9). English traders sometimes used the "scramble" method of selling slaves. In this practice, a price and time were designated beforehand, and at the signal of the owner, the buyers rushed the slaves and claimed their choices at the standard price. The bewildered victims must have been horrified. As time passed, the auction method gradually became the trusted and more prominent market practice.

Virtually all slaves faced new physical examinations during their sale and one or more brandings for identification purposes. Many found themselves separated from relatives and new-found friends. After the sale, some had to endure another voyage or a long overland journey to their final destination.

In most cases, the newly arrived slaves, often referred to as *bozals* or saltwater slaves, ended up at plantations, which, if surrounded by forest, might have given them a sense of familiarity. Their new surroundings also gave them new masters whose language was foreign to them, new companions, and a new regimen of hard labor and perpetual servitude. Many slaves faced brutal masters; others may have been luckier, but the adjustment was invariably difficult, and new arrivals often ran away from the plantations.

The initial stage of enslavement in the Americas, during which slaves adjusted to their new environment and conditions, was referred to by West Indian planters as the period of "seasoning." Thrown together with new people from many strange places, the exhausted arrivals were once more exposed to many new diseases, to which they either built up resistance or succumbed. It has been suggested that up to one-third of the slaves died during the first few years after their arrival in the New World.[19]

Notes

1. Kenneth F. Kiple, *The Caribbean Slave: A Biological History* (New York: Cambridge University Press, 1985), 57.

2. Joseph C. Miller, *Way of Death: Merchant Capitalism and the Angolan Slave Trade, 1730–1830* (Madison: University of Wisconsin Press, 1988), 384.

3. Thomas Fowell Buxton, *The African Slave Trade and Its Remedy,* (1839; reprint, London: Dawsons of Pall Mall, 1968), 99, 113; Miller, *Way of Death,* 165, 384–85.

4. Miller, *Way of Death,* 390.

5. For space on slave ships, see Herbert H. Klein, *The Atlantic Slave Trade* (New York: Cambridge University Press, 2000), 132–35.

6. Herbert S. Klein, *The Middle Passage: Comparative Studies in the Atlantic Slave Trade* (Princeton, N.J.: Princeton University Press, 1978), 228.

7. Miller, *Way of Death,* 413.

8. For illness and malnutrition during the Middle Passage, see Kiple, *The Caribbean Slave,* 57–75.

9. Klein, *Atlantic Slave Trade,* 99.

10. Philip D. Curtin, *The Atlantic Slave Trade: A Census* (Madison: University of Wisconsin Press, 1969), 278–79.

11. David Eltis, Stephen D. Behrendt, David Richardson, and Herbert S. Klein, eds., *The Trans-Atlantic Slave Trade: A Database on CD ROM* (New York: Cambridge University Press, 1999). See also Herbert S. Klein, Stanley L. Engerman, Robin Haines, and Ralph Shlomowitz, "Transoceanic Mortality: The Slave Trade in Comparative Perspective," *William and Mary Quarterly* 58, no. 1 (January 2001): 113.

12. Johannes Postma, *The Dutch in the Atlantic Slave Trade, 1600–1815* (New York: Cambridge University Press, 1990), xiii, 164, 242–43.

13. See David Richardson, "Shipboard Revolts, African Authority, and the Atlantic Slave Trade," *William and Mary Quarterly* 58, no. 1 (January 2001): 69–92.

14. Richardson, "Shipboard Revolts," 75.

15. Richardson, "Shipboard Revolts," 78–90.

16. Postma, *Dutch in the Atlantic Slave Trade,* 167–68; Robert L. Stein, *The French Slave Trade in the Eighteenth Century* (Madison: University of Wisconsin Press, 1979), 105–106.

17. Miller, *Way of Death,* 410–11.

18. Richardson, "Shipboard Revolts," 74.

19. Kiple, *The Caribbean Slave,* 64–65.

CHAPTER 3

THE STATISTICS: ORIGINS, DESTINATIONS, AND MORTALITY

Identifying the Enslaved

Who were the unfortunate forced migrants from Africa? Is it possible to find out more about their lives, their feelings, their apprehensions, and their identities? Unfortunately, hardly any firsthand accounts of their experiences survive. Most of our knowledge comes from the archival records of ship captains, merchants, and others involved in the slave trade, and these give only a glimpse of the ordeal experienced by the slaves. Only rarely is a slave identified by name, as in the case of the Asante slave Essjerrie Ettin, who led a slave rebellion in 1770 (see "Biographical Sketches"). His identity remained hidden for two centuries until archival research uncovered his name and story. A few personal accounts, including those of former slaves Olaudah Equiano, Ayuba Suleiman Diallo, and Samuel Ajayi Crowther; explorer Mungo Park; and merchants Willem Bosman and John Newton, are included in the document section of this book.

Some of the basic problems concerning the Atlantic slave trade are statistical in nature, and here the archives give us much insight. How many enslaved people were actually shipped from Africa, and how many of those arrived in the Americas? How many died during the Middle Passage, before they even departed, or shortly after their arrival? Were the slaves mostly men, as in many other migrations to the Americas, or were there many women and children on the slave ships? The answers to these questions have long been a matter of speculation, but intensive research during the past three decades has greatly enhanced our understanding of the Atlantic slave trade.

Surviving records hardly ever refer to slaves by name. They were generally identified by the number assigned to them as they boarded the ship or by the branding applied to their skin, often a symbol of the company that claimed ownership or the ship that transported them (see illustration 2). European managers of the slave trade referred to slaves in impersonal terms such as slaves, Negroes, Blacks, or heads, as in "head of cattle." By comparison, sailors were collectively referred to as hands, as in "all hands on deck," but they were individually known by name. The Portuguese and Spaniards usually identified prime slaves as *pieza de India* (literally, pieces of India), a term that measured their value as potential laborers (see document 9). Because children might die before becoming effective workers, their labor potential was lower and they were sold at a fractional value of a healthy adult. For example, a transport might consist of five hundred slaves, but 480½ *pieza*. Slaves who had mental or physical handicaps, such as blindness in one eye, missing teeth, an injured or crippled leg, or other disabilities, were often referred to as macrons (*manquerons*), meaning defective.[1]

The Search for Information

The number of Africans forced across the Atlantic has long been a matter of speculation. Estimates have ranged from fewer than four million to one hundred million, but the figure most frequently cited during the twentieth century has been from twelve to fifteen million. As Basil Davidson noted in 1961, "The short answer is that nobody knows or ever will know: either the necessary records are missing or they were never made. The best one can do is to construct an estimate from confused and incomplete data."[2] The reason for this confusing situation is that, until recently, no one had studied the traffic systematically. After the flood of publications written by British abolitionists in the eighteenth and early nineteenth centuries, the slave trade received little attention for about a century. During the 1930s, there was a brief revival of slave trade interest, especially among French scholars who started a systematic study, and an American historian who published a four-volume set of documents about the Atlantic slave trade.[3] The decolonization process and growth of the civil rights movement rekindled interest in the 1960s, but publications from this period relied heavily on abolitionist literature of the previous century rather than archival research.[4] Abolitionists, however, had not been systematic scholars. Because their goal was to change public opinion and get lawmakers to abolish first the slave trade and then slavery, they cited the most extreme cases of profits made and mortality suffered.

The vagueness about estimates and numbers in the slave trade prompted Professor Philip Curtin to examine this issue during the 1960s. His influential and frequently cited book, *The Atlantic Slave Trade: A Census*, published in 1969, examined the origins of the conflicting estimates and concluded that most were highly speculative. He set up a framework for making more reliable projections for the traffic using recent scholarship, including foreign publications and new computer technology to project slave imports from later censuses. In addition to new estimates for the volume of the traffic, Curtin examined African origins, American destinations, and mortality during the Middle Passage. Stimulated by this work, many scholars started combing the archives and publishing their findings. The Cambridge University Press Database eventually brought this information together in a general data collection and made it available in electronic form on CD in 1999.[5] This collection will be updated as new information becomes available, and will serve as a vital source in slave trade studies.

The Numbers

Curtin's estimates for the volume of the Atlantic slave trade were lower than had often been claimed. By his calculation, nearly 9.4 million enslaved Africans reached the Americas, while another 175,000 were shipped to Europe and the African Atlantic islands. Allowing for an estimated 12 to 15 percent mortality rate during the Atlantic crossing, approximately eleven million must have been shipped from Africa. Some scholars believed that Curtin's figures were too low, but as more and more data were collected, new estimates deviated only slightly.[6]

Table 3.1, which summarizes material in the Cambridge University Press Database and provides a period breakdown to show trends in the traffic, indicates that the total number of slaves exported from Africa was slightly higher than eleven million. The table does not include the approximately 175,000 slaves shipped to Europe and the African Atlantic islands during the early years of the traffic. The database identifies nearly 26,000 slaving voyages and adds estimates for

Table 3.1
Exports of Slaves from Africa by Nationality of Carrier (in thousands)

	Britain	France	Spain	Nether lands*	USA & Br. Carib.	Denmark	Portugal & Brazil	All Nations	Annual Volume
1519–1600	2.0						264.1	266.1	3.3
1601–1650	23.0			39.9			439.5	502.4	4.1
1651–1675	115.2	5.9		59.5		0.2	53.7	234.5	9.4
1676–1700	243.3	34.1		97.4		15.4	161.1	551.3	22.1
1701–1725	380.9	106.3		74.5	11.0	16.7	378.3	967.7	38.7
1726–1750	490.5	253.9		76.4	44.5	7.6	405.6	1,278.5	51.2
1751–1775	859.1	321.5	1.0	118.2	89.1	13.4	472.9	1,875.2	75.0
1776–1800	741.3	419.5	8.6	34.2	54.3	30.4	626.2	1,914.5	76.6
1801–1825	257.0	217.9	204.8	1.3	81.1	10.5	871.6	1,644.2	65.8
1826–1850		94.1	279.2				1,247.7	1,621.0	64.8
1851–1867		3.2	23.4				154.2	180.8	10.6
All Years	3,112.3	1,456.4	517	501.4	280	94.2	5,074.9	11,036.2	30.4
Percentage	28.2%	13.2%	4.7%	4.5%	2.5%	0.9%	46.0%	100.0%	

Source: David Eltis, "The Volume and Structure of the Transatlantic Slave Trade: A Reassessment," William and Mary Quarterly 58, no. 1 (January 2001): 17–31.

*Figures for the Dutch slave trade have been revised; see Johannes Postma, "A Reassessment of the Dutch Slave Trade," in Riches from Atlantic Commerce, ed. Johannes Postma and Victor Enthoven (Leiden: Brill, 2003).

another 10,000 for which specific data have not been found, primarily for the early years. As research on the slave trade continues, additional slaving voyages may be identified, which could either raise or lower the estimates, but not to a significant degree.

Carriers and Trends in the Traffic

Although at least ten nations participated as carriers, three out of every four slaves sailed on a British or Portuguese ship (see table 3.1). With 46 percent of the total, Portugal and its colonial subjects in Brazil were by far the major carriers, primarily because they transported slaves from the beginning of the traffic to its end. Portugal dominated the traffic before 1650 and again after 1807. More than half of the Portuguese slave traders operated from Brazil, a Portuguese colony that gained a degree of economic independence similar to North America's from Britain. Portuguese traders supplied the large numbers of slaves needed for Brazil's plantations and mines, and were major suppliers for Cuba during the nineteenth century. Britain was the second most active carrier, with 28 percent of the overall traffic, although its involvement was relatively short. Britain became an active participant in the seventeenth century and abolished the slave trade relatively early, in 1808. From about 1650 to 1807, however, the British clearly dominated the traffic.

France's 13 percent of the traffic went primarily to its Caribbean island colonies and also briefly to the Spanish colonies. Spain and the Netherlands were relatively minor participants, with about 4.5 percent each. Although a latecomer to the transatlantic slave trade because it lacked African trading stations, Spain established a few such stations in the nineteenth century when Cuba started growing sugarcane and demanded slave labor. The United Provinces, or Dutch Republic, was briefly a major carrier of slaves only during the 1680s, when it controlled the *asiento* trade with Spanish America by way of the island of Curaçao. Afterwards, the Dutch shipped slaves primarily to Surinam, their most important colony in the West Indies.

British North America, and later the United States, carried about 2.5 percent of the traffic, with British Caribbean traders taking a small portion of that. This small percentage may be surprising, but North Americans entered the traffic relatively late, shortly before 1700, and generally used very small ships that often carried fewer than one hundred slaves. Denmark shipped less than 1 percent of the traffic. Not mentioned in the table are Sweden, Brandenburg (Prussia), and the Spanish and Austrian Netherlands (today's Belgium), which together shipped fewer than five thousand slaves.[7]

The general flow of the Atlantic slave trade is indicated by the figures in the final columns of table 3.1. The traffic peaked between the years 1727 and 1850, when an average of more than 76,000 Africans were deported each year. Of course there were fluctuations within this time frame, and some years saw more than 100,000 slaves taken from Africa.

Origins of the Slaves

Exactly where in Africa did the slaves come from? That remains a difficult question because no records were kept on the enslaved individuals. Because many coastal regions were involved in the trade, selling slaves to the Europeans, trade slaves generally came from the interior. Studies of ethnic origins have produced some results, but family roots are difficult to trace. In a few cases, such as the celebrated effort of Alex Haley, family roots have been traced through a combination of oral family histories and archival research. The new science of DNA offers promise to such endeavors.[8] The Cambridge University Press Database provides statistical information about African coastal areas from which slave ships departed that can also help track ethnic and/or family roots. It shows that many slave ships returned to the same regions, and they often traded with the same African merchants. This suggests that transports were often made up of slaves from the same region, even if they were not of the same ethnic group.[9]

Map 3.1 is a guide to significant ports and coastal regions that played important roles in the slave trade. Table 3.2 provides a breakdown of the number of slaves exported from each region and shows that slightly more than 50 percent of Africans in the Atlantic diaspora set sail from the long coastline between Senegal and the Cameroons, the Guinea Coast.

Large numbers of slaves were exported from the Bight of Benin, as its former name "Slave Coast" signifies. It served as the exit point for 18.5 percent, or more than two million, of enslaved Africans. The Bight of Biafra was the second largest exporting region in West Africa, with over 1.5 million, followed by the Gold Coast with more than one million of the forced emigrants. The Slave Coast exported slaves from the early years of the traffic until the early nineteenth century. By contrast, the Gold Coast was primarily a gold exporting region until about 1700, when its gold deposits became depleted and the demand for slaves increased. The Bight of Biafra did not become a major exporting region until the traffic peaked during the mid–eighteenth century. The rather long coastline from Senegal to the Ivory Coast exported comparatively few slaves. The shorter distance from Senegambia to the Americas would have favored this region, but for reasons not yet clear, it exported slightly less than 10 percent of all slaves who crossed the Atlantic. West African regions displayed a general pattern in which slave exports tended to rise rapidly, maintain a high level for several years, and then drop to a low level again. This pattern cannot be explained by European demand, but must have been determined by forces or values within the specific African regions, which have not yet been fully explored.[10]

About 44 percent, or nearly five million slaves, originated from west central Africa, including the area still known as Angola and the

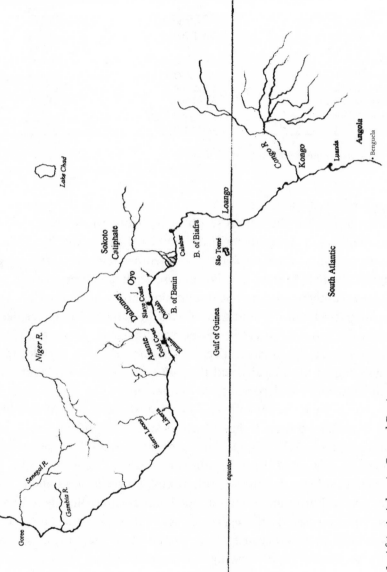

Map 3.1 Africa's Atlantic Coastal Regions

Table 3.2
African Origins

Regions	Slaves	Percent
Senegambia	497,500	4.5 %
Sierra Leone	411,700	3.7 %
Windward Coast	180,000	1.7 %
Gold Coast	1,035,200	9.4 %
Bight of Benin	2,030,600	18.4 %
Bight of Biafra	1,515,900	13.7 %
West Central Africa	4,880,500	44.2 %
Southeast Africa	484,500	4.4 %
Regions Combined	11,036,200	100 %

Source: Eltis, "Volume and Structure," 46, table 5.

region between the Congo River and Cameroon. The Portuguese primarily dominated the region south of the Congo River and exported vast numbers of slaves through the ports at Luanda and Benguela. In the area north of the Congo River (sometimes referred to as Loango), English, French, Dutch, and Portuguese traders competed with each other for captives, with no one dominating the trade. As the slave trade era progressed and demand grew, slaves were taken from ever deeper within the interior. After the traffic was abolished along the Guinea Coast in the early nineteenth century, it continued for decades in the Angola region, first legally and then illegally, perhaps explaining why such large numbers departed from that region.[11]

Slaves were also taken from southeast Africa, today's Mozambique and Tanzania, both for Indian Ocean destinations and for the Atlantic traffic. As table 3.2 illustrates, 4.4 percent of the slaves taken to the Americas originated from southeastern Africa. This area did not become significant for the Atlantic traffic, however, until about 1800, after several European nations stopped participating. Brazilian, French, and American slavers were especially active there, some legally and others as illicit traders. Because of the latter and the great distances, mortality rates tended to be very high on these voyages.[12]

American Destinations

Enslaved Africans were taken to a variety of destinations in the New World. Quite often they were shipped to ports not far from the

Table 3.3
American Destinations

Destinations	Slaves	Percent
Br. Mainland No. America	361,100	3.8%
British Leewards	304,900	3.2%
Br. Windwards and Trinidad	362,000	3.8%
Jamaica	1,077,100	11.2%
Barbados	494,200	5.2%
Guyana and Surinam	385,700	4.0%
French Windwards	305,200	3.2%
St. Domingue	787,400	8.2%
Spanish American Mainland	430,300	4.5%
Spanish Caribbean	791,900	8.3%
Dutch Caribbean	124,700	1.3%
Northeast Brazil	876,100	9.1%
Bahia	1,008,000	10.5%
Southeast Brazil	2,017,900	21.1%
Other Americas	118,700	1.2%
Africa	130,800	1.4%
All Regions	9,576,000	100.0%

Source: Eltis, "Volume and Structure," 45, table 3. Destinations to Dutch colonies have been modified; see note on table 3.1.

plantations or mines where they were put to work. Usually a short overland or riverboat trip was the final leg of the journey, but perhaps 5 to 10 percent of the slaves had to make an additional ocean voyage. This was particularly so for those shipped to transitional depots like Curaçao and Jamaica, from which they were transshipped to the Spanish colonial ports of Cartagena (Colombia), Veracruz (Mexico), and Portobelo (Panama). In addition, untold numbers of slaves were smuggled to the Caracas Coast of today's Venezuela from nearby Caribbean islands. Others were shipped from the Caribbean to North American colonies. Some were transferred within countries, from Brazilian plantations to the gold mining areas in Minas Gerais, for example, and in the United States, from the southern coast to the western cotton plantations.[13]

Of the sixteen regions in the Americas where slaves were taken, identified in table 3.3, Brazil was the most important destination. Nearly four million, or 41 percent of the slaves crossing the Atlantic, ended up in one of its three major regions. Brazil imported slaves from Africa during the entire time the Atlantic slave trade was a sizable operation. Slavery was an important institution there as late as the 1850s and was not abolished until 1888.

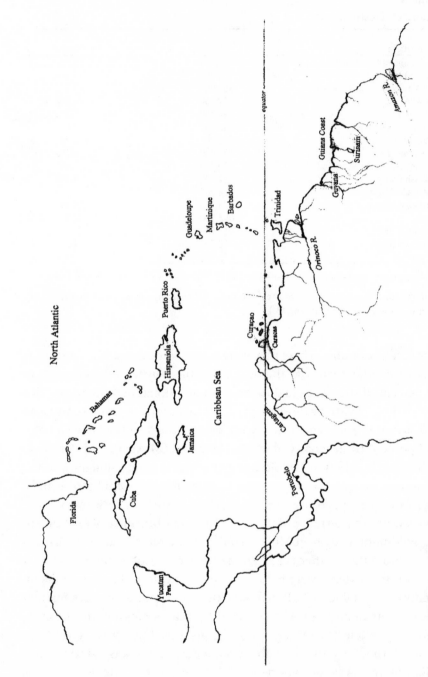

North Atlantic

Florida

Bahamas

Cuba

Yucatan Pen.

Jamaica

Hispaniola

Puerto Rico

Caribbean Sea

Guadeloupe

Martinique

Barbados

Curaçao

Caracas

Trinidad

Cartagena

Portobelo

Orinoco R.

Guyana

Guiana Coast

Surinam

Amazon R.

equator

Map 3.2 The West Indies in the Slave Trade Era

British traders took most of their transports to the first five areas listed in table 3.3, but they also shipped slaves to Spanish colonies under the *asiento* agreement. The Dutch controlled nearly all of the Guiana settlements until 1795, landing about a quarter of a million slaves in the colonies at Surinam and Guyana. They also supplied their Caribbean islands and must have re-exported more than 100,000 slaves to Spanish and French colonies by way of Curaçao and St. Eustatius (see illustration 7).

The Spanish colonies imported slightly more than 1.2 million slaves, or nearly 13 percent of the overall volume, but more than half were shipped by foreign carriers. The French Caribbean colonies took in nearly 1.1 million, or nearly 11.5 percent of the total. The vast majority of these went to St. Domingue (Haiti).[14] The slaves in the category "Other Americas" went primarily to the Danish Caribbean. The 130,000 slaves who ended up back in Africa were those taken from illicit slave ships and returned (see chapter 5).

The Cambridge University Press Database shows that a surprisingly low number, about 361,100 or 3.8 percent of all slaves transported to the New World, were taken to colonial North America and later the United States. British ships were the principal carriers to its American colonies, but North Americans got involved in the traffic during the eighteenth century, especially after the American Revolution. They tended to use smaller ships, however, and were actively engaged in taking slaves to various Caribbean islands and Guyana. During the last decades of the eighteenth century, they shipped nearly three thousand slaves to Dutch-controlled Surinam alone.[15]

Mortality during Middle Passage

One of the much-debated issues concerning the Atlantic slave trade is the death rate for slaves during the Middle Passage, only one leg of their long journey. Abolitionists cited extremely high mortality figures for slaves and sailors, and used them to denounce the slave trade as both immoral and wasteful. Because slaves were valuable investment property, ship captains kept careful records in logbooks and mortality lists of the dates and causes of death, as well as the gender and age of the deceased. These records survive for about one-fifth of the documented slave voyages and are now accessible through the Cambridge University Press

Database. They show that on average 12 percent of the enslaved did not survive the ocean crossing, though there was considerable variation from one transport to another. Before 1700, death rates tended to be higher, averaging more than 22 percent. They decreased to about 10 percent by the end of the eighteenth century, but rose again to nearly 12 percent during the years of illegal trading in the mid–nineteenth century.[16]

When compared to inflated mortality rates cited by abolitionists, these percentages may seem moderate. But these deaths occurred on voyages averaging about three months, and if extended over a yearlong period and maintaining the same death rate, the per annum mortality rate would be nearly 50 percent. Those are extremely high losses by any standard. According to ocean-mortality specialists:

> The high rates of mortality of slave ships greatly exceeded the customary death rates of populations on land, even considering those of the great human disasters such as the Black Death, the decimation of native Americans . . . , and the Irish Famine, as well as mortality on other types of sea voyages, such as those carrying indentured workers and free migrants.[17]

Considering that most of these people were in the prime of their life, between the ages of fifteen and thirty-five, these figures are even more astounding.

Mortality rates on the Middle Passage were unpredictable and varied considerably from one voyage to another. A few ships suffered no casualties at all, while others suffered catastrophic losses, especially in cases of epidemics or shipwrecks. There was little difference in slave mortality rates between carriers of different nations, except that Portugal had a lower rate of 8.6 percent, perhaps because its route between Africa and Brazil was shorter. Slave mortality rates were also affected by where a transport originated. Voyages leaving the Biafran coast registered significantly higher death rates, 17.4 percent on average, compared with rates of 9.5 percent for departures from west-central Africa. The vast majority of these transports went to Brazil, which may explain these lower rates. The high Biafran rates are baffling; perhaps they reflect a larger presence of vulnerable children among the transports or conditions in the African interior such as famine and epidemics.[18]

High mortality rates during the Middle Passage were usually blamed on conditions aboard the slave ships, and there is no doubt that crowding spread contagious diseases quickly. Intestinal disorders such as dysentery were the most common killers, often appearing in epidemic proportions. These ailments, along with tropical diseases such as malaria and yellow fever were responsible for about 70 percent of the casualties. Smallpox and scurvy also killed slaves, particularly before the mid–eighteenth century. Respiratory illnesses, heart attacks, suicide (jumping overboard or refusing to eat), revolts, storms, shipwrecks, attacks by pirates, and fights among slaves were also listed as causes of death.[19]

It has been argued that unusually long voyages and extreme crowding, "tight packing," were responsible for high death rates. Extremely long ocean crossings did deplete water and food resources, but usually shipowners took on twice the amount of supplies they needed for an average voyage. Epidemics often claimed many lives regardless of the extent of crowding.[20] Conditions prior to boarding could also be important. Germs could be carried aboard undetected, and slaves weakened from malnutrition and other hardships were more susceptible to disease. Larger slave ships usually had a doctor and surgeons onboard, but they could do very little to prevent or cure disease. As the eighteenth century progressed, traders learned that consumption of citrus fruit could prevent scurvy, and ship doctors also began to inoculate against smallpox. These measures contributed to the decline of mortality rates on slave ships.

Unnecessary cruelty on the part of slave traders may occasionally have contributed to slave mortality. During the British parliamentary debates to end the slave trade at the beginning of the nineteenth century, abolitionists introduced the notorious case of the slave ship *Zong* in 1781. After an unusually long voyage from Africa, the ship had nearly run out of water and was suffering much illness and loss of life. Its captain, Luke Collingwood, ordered 133 sick or dying slaves to be thrown into the sea. After the captain made an insurance claim on the loss, it became a court case in which the captain claimed that his orders were necessary to save the lives of others, although the captain's mate had objected to the action and it rained shortly after the last group of slaves were thrown overboard. When abolitionists spread news of the case, it aroused support for their cause among the public as well as in Parliament.[21] Such incidents were not widespread, however, and they ran counter to regulations and to the financial interest of slave ship officers who usually received bonuses for delivering slaves alive.

Gender and Age

In major human migrations to distant areas, men have usually outnumbered women and children. This was true for migrations involving indentured servants, convicts, or free emigrants, and also for the forced migration from Africa to the Americas. During the early years of the slave trade to Spanish America, the *asiento* contracts (document 9) set the pattern of allowing one female for every two male slaves, and this ratio was fairly well maintained. European traders tried to limit the number of women and children, despite the lower purchase price on the African coast, because planters and miners in the New World wanted slaves for heavy labor. When planters realized that women could work effectively on plantations, and as demand for slaves grew, they purchased both women and children more readily. The number of children under age fifteen was initially quite small on slave ships, but it increased significantly after 1700. Boys became particularly more numerous in the transports.[22]

The preference for men was not only determined by American demands, but also by conditions in Africa. A large number of men were enslaved as prisoners of war. The flow of slaves to the Middle East and North Africa showed a preference for female slaves, and African polygamous marriages tended to produce a surplus of unmarried men, making more male slaves available on the Atlantic coast.

African professor Ugo Nwokeji claims that cultural determinants also affected gender ratios in the slave trade. Whereas women played a crucial role in agriculture in other areas of Africa; among the Igbo and the Ibibio of Biafra, yam was the staple food and was "cultivated exclusively by men and regarded as the king of crops," which may explain why so many more women were enslaved and exported from that particular region.[23] This is confirmed by the Cambridge University Press Database, which shows that slave exports from the Bight of Biafra included 45 percent women during the period 1650–1700. While this percentage declined afterwards, it remained much higher than in other export regions. This region also relied much less on prisoners of war as a source for slaves. Recent studies confirm that conditions in Africa had a far greater impact on many aspects of the slave trade than was previously thought.

Slave Ship Crews

For crews and officers alike, service on slave ships was one of the last jobs a mariner wanted. Desperation and hunger drove many men to sign on; others were often lured aboard a ship while drunk. Perhaps sailors were aware that slave ships were unhealthy places. Several studies indicate that death rates among slave ship crews were often higher than among the slaves. Perhaps this was because they were onboard much longer than the slaves. Their voyages consisted of five stages: Europe to Africa, African coastal stay, Middle Passage, American port call, return voyage. The first and last legs of the voyage without slaves were the least demanding and life-threatening. Most dangerous for crew members was the African coast, where almost half of the deaths (45.8 percent) occurred. The next most dangerous legs were the Middle Passage and the call at American ports, registering 27.9 and 25.2 percent mortality respectively. According to slave trade scholar Stephen Behrendt: "The primary aim of merchants in the late eighteenth century was to minimize slave deaths in the middle passage to ensure a profitable voyage. Minimizing crew mortality was a secondary consideration."[24] Tropical illnesses were the greatest threats to European mariners. While crew members were less confined than the slaves, the unhygienic conditions of the slave ship exposed everyone aboard to contagious diseases.

While shipboard life of crew members was obviously better than that of slaves, it was far from pleasant. Although spared the filthy quarters below, sailors often slept wherever they could find a place on deck. Officers undoubtedly had better living quarters, but heavily salted food and excessive drinking further endangered the sailors' health. Corporal punishment for infractions of the captain's absolute authority could be brutal and sometimes fatal. All ranks suffered heavy death rates, but they were highest among the ships' doctors and surgeons because of their direct contact with sick persons.

Some crews were so devastated by losses that they could barely keep their ships sailing. In 1723, after losing all its crew members, the slave ship *Petronella Alida* and its forty surviving slaves were finally taken over by a Portuguese ship. In 1773, the slave ship *Stad en Lande* lost nearly all its crew members, and the captain and four surviving sailors were barely able to sail it into the Surinam River.[25] Heavy losses of crew members on British slave ships became one of the main arguments used by abolitionists to end the traffic. The British Parliament eventually passed a number of acts regulating space requirements and improving slave-crew ratios, which lowered mortality among slaves and crews.

Conclusion

Over the past three decades, the Atlantic slave trade has become a focal point of study, and scholars from across the world have uncovered much new information about it. Carefully maintained records of the traffic, preserved in various archives, suggest that participants considered it a legitimate business. Before the end of the eighteenth century, few people condemned the slave trade or urged its abolition, and many regarded it as either a normal business or at worst a necessary evil. Ironically, much of our knowledge of the slave trade is a result of that attitude, for if their business records had not been kept, we would know very little about it.

Notes

1. Philip D. Curtin, *The Atlantic Slave Trade: A Census* (Madison: University of Wisconsin Press, 1969), 22. See also document 9.

2. Basil Davidson, *The African Slave Trade: Precolonial History, 1450–1850* (Boston, Mass.: Little, Brown Co., 1961), 79. A hardcover edition of the book was published in 1961 under the title *Black Mother.*

3. Elisabeth Donnan, *Documents Illustrative of the Slave Trade to America,* 4 vols. (Washington, D.C.: Carnegie Institution, 1931); Robert L. Stein, *The French Slave Trade in the Eighteenth Century* (Madison: University of Wisconsin Press, 1979), xvii.

4. Good examples of this genre are Basil Davidson's *Black Mother,* and Daniel P. Mannix and Malcolm Cowley's *Black Cargoes* (New York: Viking Press, 1962).

5. David Eltis, Stephen D. Behrendt, David Richardson, and Herbert S. Klein, eds., *The Trans-Atlantic Slave Trade: A Database on CD ROM* (New York: Cambridge University Press, 1999). The database was originally sponsored by the Du Bois Institute at Harvard University.

6. Curtin, *The Atlantic Slave Trade,* xvi and 268; Paul E. Lovejoy, "The Volume of the Atlantic Slave Trade: A Synthesis," *Journal of African History* 22, no. 4 (1982): 473–501.

7. David Eltis, "The Volume and Structure of the Transatlantic Slave Trade: A Reassessment," *William and Mary Quarterly* 58, no. 1 (January 2001): 17–31.

8. Alex Haley, *Roots: The Saga of an American Family* (New York: Doubleday, 1976). Pearl Duncan has been studying the use of DNA in tracing African roots; see her Web site, http://www.pearlduncan.com.

9. Eltis, "Volume and Structure," 32.

10. Eltis, "Volume and Structure," 31–35.

11. See Joseph Miller's *Way of Death: Merchant Capitalism and the Angolan Slave Trade, 1730–1830* (Madison: University of Wisconsin Press, 1988), which focuses on the slave trade from this area.

12. Herbert S. Klein, *The Atlantic Slave Trade* (New York: Cambridge University Press, 1999), 70.

13. Eltis, "Volume and Structure," 35–36.

14. See David Geggus, "The French Slave Trade: An Overview," *William and Mary Quarterly* 58, no. 1 (January 2001): 125–26.

15. Johannes Postma, "Surinam and Its Atlantic Connections, 1667–1795," in *Riches from Atlantic Commerce* (Leiden: Brill, 2003), chapter 11.

16. For mortality statistics, see Herbert S. Klein, Stanley L. Engerman, Robin Haines, and Ralph Shlomowitz, "Transoceanic Mortality: The Slave Trade in Comparative Perspective," *William and Mary Quarterly* 58, no. 1 (January 2001): 93–118.

17. Klein, Engerman, Haines, and Shlomowitz, "Transoceanic Mortality," 96.

18. Ibid., 93–117.

19. Klein, *The Atlantic Slave Trade*, 151; Johannes Postma, *The Dutch in the Atlantic Slave Trade, 1600–1815* (New York: Cambridge University Press, 1990), 244.

20. Klein, *The Atlantic Slave Trade*, 99.

21. Donnan, *Documents*, vol. 2: 555–57.

22. G. Ugo Nwokeji, "African Perception of Gender and the Slave Traffic," *William and Mary Quarterly* 58, no. 1 (January 2001): 58–64.

23. Ibid., 59.

24. Stephen D. Behrendt, "Crew Mortality in the Transatlantic Slave Trade in the Eighteenth Century," in *Routes to Slavery*, ed. David Eltis and David Richardson (London: Frank Cass, 1997), 66.

25. Postma, *The Dutch in the Atlantic Slave Trade*, 157.

CHAPTER 4

TRADE IN PEOPLE: PROFITS, LOSSES, AND CONSEQUENCES

The Slave Trade in the World Economy

The Atlantic slave trade was not an isolated business, but an intricate part of the evolving modern world economy. Spices and textiles from Asia, precious metals and tropical produce from the Americas, gold and labor from Africa, and capital and technology from Europe were transported across the oceans in an integrated global economic network. Consumers around the world wanted merchandise and commodities from elsewhere. Africans were eager to buy manufactured goods in exchange for their natural resources, such as gold and ivory, as well as slaves. The slave trade became an integral part of this process, as historian Barbara Solow describes so vividly:

> It was slavery that made the empty lands of the western hemisphere valuable producers of commodities and valuable markets for Europe and North America: What moved in the Atlantic in these centuries was predominantly slaves . . . [and] the goods and services purchased on the earnings of slave products. To give just one example, by the late seventeenth century, the New England merchant, the Madeiran vintner, the Barbadian planter, the English manufacturer, the English slave trader, and the African slave trader were joined in an intricate web of interdependent economic activity.[1]

Europeans functioned as intermediaries and transporters of the world's products, and their advanced shipping technology and financial institutions, such as insurance brokerages, banks, and business firms, gave them tremendous advantages. But they also competed with each other, both as individual firms and as national entities, for the benefits that this economic system offered. The enormous investment risks in long-distance trade drove European governments and merchants into cooperative ventures, giving rise to joint-stock firms such as the Royal African and West India Companies. Several European governments encouraged these enterprises in order to gain territory and enlarge their national wealth. They also tried to exclude foreign merchants from their colonial markets through a system called mercantilism. Some subsidized overseas business ventures, but they also taxed their own merchants in order to increase government revenues. The merchant community often protested against such burdens and restrictions, and the notion of free trade gained considerable support during the eighteenth century, easing restrictions and encouraging greater competition within national communities. Adam Smith (1723–90), Scottish economic theorist and author of *Wealth of Nations,* was an influential advocate of free trade. Although Smith opposed the slave trade, it is ironic that the slave trade and the free trade developed simultaneously.[2]

Markets and long-distance trade were important in African societies long before the slave trade, as evidenced by trans-Saharan caravans and other regional trading networks. Therefore, tying into the emerging global system was not difficult, despite linguistic and cultural differences with Europeans. Trading contacts between Europeans and Africans were hampered, however, by the lack of standardized measurements. European countries employed a variety of monetary units and weight measurements, at times more than one within a country. The small Dutch Republic, for example, used the guilder as its money standard, but its southern Zeeland province used the Flemish pound. Not until Napoleon's empire in the early nineteenth century did the metric system become the uniform standard for much of continental Europe, and even then Britain kept its own systems.

Trade with Africa added complications. Each region of Africa had its own measures and market routines. On the Gold Coast, gold was the standard of value, which Europeans willingly adopted in their dealings with that region. Indian Ocean cowry shells were an important medium of exchange on the Slave Coast, but occasionally business transactions were calculated in terms of the value of a slave. For example, in 1709, West India Company officials figured that expanding the trade lodge at Ouidah on the Slave Coast would cost twelve to fourteen slaves. In other areas, copper or metal bars were standards of value in African-European commerce.

The Complexity of the Traffic

Compared with most shuttle trades between one port and another, the Atlantic slave traffic was extremely complicated, primarily because of its triangular nature and involuntary human cargo. The slave trade required careful and systematic planning because it involved at least three commercial zones. Outfitting a slave ship involved hiring a crew twice the size of ordinary merchant voyages, and one suitable for the tropics. Because different regions in Africa demanded different goods, merchandise had to be selected according to the region where slaves would be purchased. Large quantities of provisions needed to be loaded for feeding the crew and enslaved passengers during the voyage. These included beans, biscuits, and salted meats, large amounts of drinking water, and an assortment of alcoholic beverages. Additional provisions were generally bought in Africa. Rice could be obtained in Senegambia, maize (Indian corn) on the Gold Coast and the Bay of Benin, and yams in the Bay of Biafra. Captains sailing to Angola could not count on buying African food, because it was generally in short supply there. All these purchases needed to be planned carefully in accordance with the seasons and availability, and cost was an important consideration for all areas.[3]

Market conditions and demands in the Americas were also considerations. To fetch the best prices for slaves, ships needed to arrive just before or during the harvest season, when the demand for labor was greatest. Crop seasons varied from the tropics to the temperate zones, and ship captains could sometimes plan or alter their course to sell slaves at more than one location, but changes cost time and put the vulnerable human cargoes at risk. Political, economic, and weather conditions also needed to be considered. To sail into the Caribbean during the hurricane season would not only increase risks, but also raise the cost of insurance coverage. Historian Stephen Behrendt best sums up the complexity of this process:

> Transaction cycles on three continents dictated decision making, because merchants wanted slaving ventures to depart from and arrive at markets in Europe, Africa, and the Americas at optimal

times, coordinating slave supply and demand. The choice of African market largely determined the quantity of trading goods and provisions to load in England [or elsewhere], the number of slaves to purchase, the anticipated duration of trading on the African coast, and the predicted season of arrival in the Americas.[4]

Because of the different monetary standards and measurements, the trade in slaves on the African coast was conducted primarily through a barter system. African regions generally specialized in their own unique items for export, and each of the highly diverse population groups had its own distinct appreciation for imported goods. African preferences had to be taken seriously or European traders might lose out to competitors.

Most experienced European merchants developed lasting connections with African merchants, establishing a degree of mutual trust and friendship. To purchase large numbers of slaves, European traders usually negotiated agreements with prominent African merchants and kings, agreeing on the price per slave beforehand, as explained by Willem Bosman in document 5. Free traders commonly bartered for slaves at various places along the coast, exchanging an assortment of goods for one or a few slaves at a time.[5]

European Trade Goods

Europeans traded a large assortment of goods, including a variety of textiles, alcoholic beverages, guns and gunpowder, iron and copper bars, tools, utensils, and other household and luxury items, including mirrors and beads. Copper and iron bars from Sweden were desired in the Bay of Biafra region. Indian Ocean cowry shells shipped to Europe from the Maldive Islands were used on the Slave Coast, as payment for slaves and as currency and ornaments. John Thornton, scholar of African history, concludes that none of these were "essential commodities," that Africans could produce most of these items themselves, and that "Africa's trade with Europe was largely moved by prestige, fancy, changing taste, and a desire for variety."[6] They were primarily luxuries for the wealthier Africans. Brazilian and North American slave traders added more luxuries such as tobacco, sugar, and rum to the mix of merchandise sold to Africans.

Textiles of enormous variety comprised more than half of the merchandise on European slave ships. Many of these fabrics were manufactured in various European countries, including linens from the German states, but a significant portion consisted of expensive silk and cotton fabrics from Asia. Like cowry shells, these Asian textiles were shipped to Europe, and from there to Africa. At the end of the eighteenth century, the British started producing large quantities of cotton textiles for export to Africa. Contrary to earlier notions, slaves were not bought with cheap trinkets, but with expensive merchandise. According to historian Herbert Klein, these trade goods were "costly manufactured products or high-priced imports from other countries or even other continents . . . more valuable than the ship, the wages of the crew, and food supplies combined."[7]

Trade with Europe provided livelihoods for many Africans. Some had jobs as rowers and interpreters; others grew or transported provisions for the slave ships. Many Africans became dependent on the merchandise brought by Europeans, and some became addicted to consumer items such as alcoholic beverages, sugar, and tobacco. Imported luxuries often increased the prestige of powerful African rulers and merchants. Imported guns and gunpowder increased their power and enabled them to enslave more of their neighbors or enemies. In the early years of Euro-African contacts, Africans purchased these items with a variety of African-produced commodities, including gold, ivory, and beeswax. Before the end of the seventeenth century, gold was, in fact, the most highly valued export item from West Africa.[8] However, as sources of gold and ivory diminished, and the taste for imported consumer goods increased, Africans increasingly paid for imports with slaves. Historian Joseph Miller describes the practice as follows:

> Textiles and other prestige goods, new, scarce, and valuable in their nearly infinite variety, created opportunities when they first arrived but then turned into burdens that borrowers had to repay in people. Guns backed coercive methods of claiming dependents whom masters would rather have retained at home. Criminals employed firearms to seize . . . goods . . . for themselves.[9]

Pricing Slaves

Prices paid for slaves varied greatly, in Africa as well as in the Americas. Several conditions influenced this, but supply and demand were essential. Although quite stable and relatively low until the end of the seventeenth century, prices increased considerably as demand for slaves grew, especially after 1750. Because the use of multiple currencies and changing currency values over time make specific prices rather meaningless, comparing the price paid for slaves with other rates might be more useful. Before the price inflation during the eighteenth century, the average price paid for a slave on the African coast was about the same as the monthly salary of a ship captain, or half a year's wages of a sailor on a slave ship. But by the end of the eighteenth century, the growing demand for slaves pushed prices well above these levels.[10]

Other circumstances also caused variations in slave prices. Women slaves generally sold for about 10 to 20 percent less than men slaves, and children at fractional values of adults. Slaves from Angola and the Bay of Biafra generally sold for less than those from the Gold Coast and the Slave Coast. Prices were often influenced by the timing of a ship's arrival in Africa or in the West. A transport that arrived in the West during the harvest season invariably sold quickly and at inflated prices. But an epidemic in the African export region or aboard ship often delayed disembarkation and lowered the price of slaves in that transport. Warfare and famine in an African export region could increase the supply of slaves and thus lower prices. If prices of slave-grown commodities dropped, or if finances were scarce, slave prices invariably fell and slave ships often had to seek better prices at other markets. Such shifts in ventures, however, generally resulted in losses rather than profits.[11] On average, though, slaves sold in the Americas for about three times their purchase price in Africa.

The Question of Profits

The question of profitability in the slave trade has been and undoubtedly will continue to be a subject of debate among economic historians for a long time. As anti-slavery sentiment grew and people no longer viewed the slave trade as a normal enterprise, they assumed that profits must have been very high to lure participants into such an inhumane business. Commentators often seized on individual cases of exorbitant profits as typical of the traffic. In 1944, Eric Williams, prime minister of Trinidad and Tobago (1962–81), wrote the thought-provoking book *Capitalism and Slavery*, which claimed that the Industrial Revolution was built on capital earned in the Atlantic slave trade and the slave systems in the Americas.[12] However, as more information has became available after extensive research since 1970, the so-called "Williams Thesis" has lost much support in scholarly circles, although a few scholars still claim a profit range for slave traders in excess of 25 percent.[13]

Just as mortality rates during the Middle Passage varied greatly, so did financial gains in the traffic. If everything turned out favorably, a slave trader might double his investment. Fortunate timing, agreeable markets, a quick and expedient ocean crossing, absence of epidemics, and low mortality could all contribute to a profitable voyage. But the reverse usually resulted in serious financial losses. An analysis of the financial outcomes of 159 Dutch slaving voyages during the eighteenth century shows that 113 profited by at least 5 percent, including two exceptionally high profit rates of 88 and 37 percent. Fourteen of the transports came out about even, and thirty-two incurred losses; the two worst performers lost 37 and 48 percent. While the overall average was about 5 percent, because most voyages took more than a year to complete, annual gains were barely 3 percent. Were these low profits the reason the Dutch virtually abandoned the slave trade during the 1770s, or were the company reports inaccurate? Many other participating nations seem to have been more successful. Average profits of 10 percent were regarded as good investment returns at that time, and the dominant British slave traders appear to have approached profits of that size. Complex as the traffic was, there seems to have been a "high initial cost of entrance," which gave large, well-financed, and experienced companies an advantage at making sizable profits.[14]

Transporting slaves across the Atlantic was an expensive enterprise. Including the time needed to outfit a ship, slave voyages often lasted more than a year. Shipping a large group of unwilling passengers who might revolt at any opportunity required a crew twice the size needed for a regular commercial ship. Insurance tended to be quite high to cover the value of the ship, merchandise, and human cargo. Large quantities of food and other provisions, mostly for the Middle Passage, had to be purchased and boarded. Several permits had to be purchased and kept aboard to provide legitimacy and protection for the voyage, and numerous other duties and fees had to be paid at every port of call. Broker and pilot fees and customary presents to prominent African rulers and merchants had to be paid. Wages for carriers and boatmen who transported slaves and provisions, fees for auctioneers and announcers, as well as duties to officials, churches, and funds for the poor were collected at many ports in the Americas. Individually, these fees may have been modest, but together they added up to a considerable expense (see documents 5, 8, and 11).

However, while such expenses cut into a firm's profits, the slave trade provided other indirect benefits to a country's economy not readily discernable on a firm's balance sheet—including bonuses received by ship officers for delivering slaves alive, and wages earned by officers, sailors, and others employed in building and provisioning slave ships, and by managers and factory workers who produced merchandise for the trade. Although generally not considered in studies of slave trade profitability, profits from commodities produced by slave labor and jobs created for processing them in Europe contributed to the economies of slave trade nations. To calculate all the indirect benefits is nearly impossible, and there is also a danger of exaggeration.

Impact of the Slave Trade

The enslaved Africans were obviously the greatest victims of the Atlantic slave trade. Even if they survived the crossing, their lives were invariably cut short and would be filled with endless labor and a hopeless future. Their offspring were condemned to the same fate, and when freedom finally came, they suffered the dehumanizing injustice of racism, propagated by slavery.[15]

African societies also suffered from the diaspora, although some rulers and merchants reaped benefits. Several years ago, the Ghanaian scholar Adu Boahen summed up the negative consequences for Africa, including the following: Large numbers of its young men and women, most in the prime of their life, were carried off, never to return. Because the initial enslavement was largely carried out by Africans and orchestrated by men in leadership positions, the slave trade undermined the very foundation of traditional political institutions and gave rise to warlords and new states that often concentrated their efforts on hunting people. It also weakened judicial systems by creating bogus excuses to condemn men to slavery. Merchants' preoccupation with trade in humans stymied the development of traditional industries.[16]

Another negative effect of the Atlantic slave trade was the growth of slavery in West Africa. As African leaders increasingly enslaved people for export, they also retained more slaves for themselves, especially after many European countries stopped participating in the traffic and the demand for slaves declined. By the mid–nineteenth century, there may have been as many slaves in West Africa as in the Americas.[17]

Central Africa was perhaps most thoroughly impacted by the slave trade. Joseph Miller describes a gradually eastward-moving "slaving frontier," spreading war and revolution as it advanced. Growing indebtedness to Europeans forced Africans ever deeper into the interior in search of captives. New leaders who were more efficient at "harvesting slaves" replaced traditional leaders, such as kings of the Kongo. Occasionally, drought contributed to further enslavement and increased mortality among the enslaved.

Many people threatened by enslavement hid in the wilderness, and numerous captives escaped from the coffles on their way to the coast. In spite of the chaos created by the slave trade and the high export figures from the region, slaving itself probably did not "deplete the population of the region in the long run," according to Miller.[18] The African diaspora undoubtedly contributed to depopulation in some regions, but the export of captives took place over several centuries. Even if losses in some years exceeded 100,000 people, natural increases seem to have compensated, and Africa's population in general does not appear to have declined during the slave trade era. Specific areas were subjected to wars and slave raids for several years, reducing the population through enslavement and flight, but as peace returned and slave raiders moved on, the escapees eventually returned and the population gradually regained its former demographic levels.

During the era of the Atlantic slave trade, another development took place that caused a worldwide population explosion and profoundly affected Africa. As Europeans made the oceans into highways, they carried not only diseases from one continent to another, but also life-sustaining food crops. The spread of American food crops stimulated population growth in both Europe and Africa at the very time the Atlantic slave trade accelerated. Fifty million people emigrated from Europe to the Americas in less than a century, and the European population still registered an increase. Starting in the sixteenth century, Africans also adopted several American food crops, especially maize, manioc (cassava), and sweet potatoes. Biohistorian Alfred Crosby Jr. explains the link between this population increase and the slave trade:

As for the influence of these crops before 1850, we might hypothe-
size that the increased food production enabled the slave trade to
go on as long as it did without pumping the black well of Africa
dry. The Atlantic slave traders drew many, perhaps most, of their
cargos from the rain forest areas, precisely those areas where American crops enabled heavier settlement than ever before.[19]

The impact of the slave trade on Europe was perhaps less notice-
able than in either Africa or the Americas. The profits gained by Europeans through the slave trade are still being disputed, but they were
probably less than has often been assumed. No doubt, some captains
and investors earned a fortune in the traffic, but nations as a whole
might have been better off devoting their energies and investments to
other business enterprises. Some historians have argued that African
trade was far less significant to Europe, and was relatively in decline
compared to other international commercial branches.[20]

The Western Hemisphere was profoundly impacted by the influx
of forced immigrants from Africa. Nearly every region in the Americas
imported African slaves and exploited them and their descendants economically. In several Caribbean islands and in the Guiana region,
descendants of African slaves became the majority population. Perhaps
a third of Brazil's population has some African roots. The overall nature
and impact of the Atlantic slave trade is perhaps best summarized by
Klein:

> The economic ties between Asia, Europe, Africa, and America
> clearly involved a web of relationships that spans the globe. At the
> heart of this system was a Europe committed to consuming Ameri-
> can plantation crops at an ever expanding rate, crops that ranged
> from luxuries to basic necessities within the European population.
> Until European immigrants replaced them in the late nineteenth
> century, it was African slaves who enabled this consumption revo-
> lution to occur. Without that labor most of America would never
> have developed at the pace it did.[21]

Notes

1. Barbara L. Solow, ed., *Slavery and the Rise of the Atlantic System* (New
York: Cambridge University Press, 1991), 1.

2. Adam Smith, *An Inquiry into the Nature and Causes of Wealth of Nations* (1776; reprint, New York: Modern Library, 1937); David Eltis, *The Rise of African Slavery in the Americas* (New York: Cambridge University Press, 2000), 2; David Brion Davis, *The Problem of Slavery in Western Culture* (Ithaca, N.Y.: Cornell University Press, 1966), 433–38.

3. See Stephen D. Behrendt, "Markets, Transaction Cycles, and Profit: Merchant Decision Making in the British Slave Trade," *William and Mary Quarterly* 58, no. 1 (January 2001): 201.

4. Behrendt, "Markets, Transaction Cycles, and Profit," 201.

5. For Euro-African commercial relations, see John Thornton, *Africa and Africans in the Making of the Atlantic World, 1400–1800*, 2d ed. (New York: Cambridge University Press, 1998), 43–71.

6. Thornton, *Africa and Africans in the Making of the Atlantic World*, 45.

7. Herbert S. Klein, *The Atlantic Slave Trade* (New York: Cambridge University Press, 1999), 98–100. The role of British cotton textiles is explained by Joseph E. Inikori, "Slavery and the Revolution in Cotton Textile Production in England," in *The Atlantic Slave Trade: Effects on Economies . . . ,*" ed. Joseph E. Inikori and Stanley L. Engerman (Durham, N.C.: Duke University Press, 1992), 145–81.

8. Johannes Postma, "West African Exports and the Dutch West India Company, 1675–1731," *Economisch en Sociaal-Historisch Jaarboek* 36 (1973): 53–74.

9. Joseph C. Miller, *Way of Death: Merchant Capitalism and the Angolan Slave Trade, 1730–1830* (Madison: University of Wisconsin Press, 1988), 135–36.

10. Philip D. Curtin, *The Atlantic Slave Trade: A Census* (Madison: University of Wisconsin Press, 1969), 270; Johannes Postma, *The Dutch in the Atlantic Slave Trade, 1600–1815* (New York: Cambridge University Press, 1990), 154, 269.

11. Klein, *The Atlantic Slave Trade*, 107–8; Behrendt, "Markets, Transaction Cycles, and Profit," 171.

12. Eric Williams, *Capitalism and Slavery* (Chapel Hill: University of North Carolina Press, 1944). Williams placed the emphasis on the slave trade, although the two systems are clearly interwoven.

13. Stanley L. Engerman, "The Slave Trade and British Capital Formation: A Comment on the Williams Thesis," *Business History Review* 46 (1972): 430–43. The debate between several historians is illustrated in a series of articles in *The Journal of Economic History* 43 (1983): 693–729.

14. Postma, *The Dutch in the Atlantic Slave Trade*, 278–80; Klein, *The Atlantic Slave Trade*, 98–99.

15. The issue of racism is treated in chapter 6.

16. Adu Boahen, *Problems in African History* (Harlow, U.K.: Longman, 1987), 113. See also Miller, *Way of Death*, 116–17, 123.

17. Paul E. Lovejoy, "The Impact of the Atlantic Slave Trade on Africa: A Review of the Literature," *Journal of African History* 30 (1989): 389–92.

18. Miller, *Way of Death,* 105–6, 122, 140–57, 274, 385.

19. See Alfred W. Crosby, *The Columbian Exchange: Biological and Cultural Consequences of 1492* (Westport, Conn.: Greenwood Press, 1972), 165–88.

20. David Eltis and Lawrence C. Jennings, "Trade between Western Africa and the Atlantic World in the Pre-Colonial Era," *American Historical Review* 43, no. 4 (1988): 936–59.

21. Klein, *The Atlantic Slave Trade,* 101–2.

CHAPTER 5

THE STRUGGLE TO END THE ATLANTIC SLAVE TRADE

Throughout human history, most labor was coerced in one way or another, and there was little criticism of the various systems of bondage because they were considered necessary. Condemnation of slavery increased steadily during the eighteenth century, until public attitudes shifted in favor of abolishing the slave trade in the nineteenth century. The underlying causes of abolition have been debated for many years. For more than a century, British abolitionists were given primary credit for the shift in attitude, but after Eric Williams published his *Capitalism and Slavery* in 1944, his theory of economic causation of abolition was widely accepted. Since the 1970s, however, more balanced and multi-causal interpretations have become prominent.[1]

The Enlightenment and Reform

As the volume of the Atlantic slave trade reached unprecedented levels during the second half of the eighteenth century, important developments were taking place in the world, and particularly in Europe. The world population started to grow dramatically, and a profound change in attitude took place among European intellectuals that was later referred to as the Enlightenment, or the Age of Reason. By the end of the century, the Industrial Revolution, with all its technological innovations, production increases, and urbanization, took off in England and spread to the European continent and across the Atlantic. Influenced by the scientific revolution of the previous century, advocates of the Enlightenment, the so-called *philosophes,* popularized the new scientific notions and advanced a wide range of ideas that under-

mined established customs and authorities. This fresh outlook encouraged greater confidence in human reason and the ability to alter society
in harmony with the forces of nature and human preference. Traditional
ways of governing and existing social mores were challenged, and long-
standing philosophies and theological beliefs were increasingly questioned.

The most optimistic advocates of the Enlightenment believed that
endless progress was a possibility. As their writings influenced public
opinion, they unwittingly laid the foundation for political and social
unrest during the 1760–1848 period that helped shape our modern
world.[2] These events and ideas spawned the new ideologies of democ-
racy, nationalism, liberalism, conservatism, and socialism. The new way
of thinking encouraged individualism and free enterprise, which favored
wage labor over slave labor.

Enlightenment advocates often encouraged social as well as political reform. Their ideal was to create a better world, making social
injustice and exploitation targets for reform. Reformers called for
improvement in the deplorable conditions in prisons and institutions
for the mentally ill. Freedom, equality, and brotherhood became slogans
for democratic revolutions that swept through Europe and the Americas. Some *philosophes* demanded equality for women. Several attacked
slavery and the slave trade as inhumane. A new appreciation of nature
and the natural world gave rise to such notions as the "noble savage,"
and for some, "primitive" and "natural" acquired positive meanings.
This new intellectual environment encouraged anti-slavery sentiments.

The Abolition Movement

Before the second half of the eighteenth century, only a few solitary voices condemned slavery. Philosophers and religious authorities
had defended slavery and other forms of human bondage as justified by
tradition and scripture. The medieval law codes of Spain, the *Sieta par-
tides*, attempted to ease legal restrictions on slaves, but the great expansion of slavery across the Atlantic exacerbated the plight of its victims.
Enlightenment ideas and the anti-slavery movement held unprecedented hope for the enslaved. David Brion Davis calls the eighteenth-
century change of attitude "a shift in moral consciousness":

What was unprecedented by the 1760s and early 1770s was the emergence of a widespread conviction that New World slavery symbolized all the forces that threatened the true destinies of man. . . . The emergence of an international anti-slavery opinion represented a momentous turning point in the evolution of man's moral perception.[3]

After 1760, most Enlightenment advocates in France and England condemned slavery as an unnatural and evil system that needed to be abolished. The French social theorist Jean-Jacques Rousseau (1712–78) expressed his opposition to slavery in 1762, saying that there was no such thing as a right to own slaves. "The words *slave* and *right* contradict each other, and are mutually exclusive," he wrote.[4] In 1770, the French priest-*philosophe* Abbé Raynal (1713–96) anticipated a slave-led rebellion. "Liberty," he said, "is the right which nature has given to every one to dispose of himself according to his will." His words seemed prophetic when a great slave rebellion broke out in the French colony of St. Domingue in 1792. Increasingly, slavery was viewed as unnatural and morally objectionable, and by the end of the century, virtually every philosopher condemned it.

The Religious Impulse

Many Enlightenment spokesmen were secular in their outlook and often critical of state-affiliated churches, dominated by society's ruling elite. Many religious leaders sought changes within the established churches. Failing at this, they established separate denominations such as the Society of Friends (Quakers), Methodism, and other sects that had a positive and optimistic view of human nature. As early as 1720, one of these "evangelical" ministers stated: "God has implanted in our very Frame and Make, a compassionate sense of the Sufferings and Misfortunes of other People." Such ideas emanated from the concept that people are basically benevolent, or good.[5] Many evangelicals reacted against the Calvinist notion of human depravity, and instead believed in human perfectibility. Their religious calling included making the world better, instead of escaping it. Their moral responsibility called them to advocate social change, and many became active abolitionists.

The religious community that most actively advocated the abolition of slavery, both in England and the United States, was the Society
of Friends, or the Quakers. Like other people of their time, many
Quakers owned slaves and some participated in the slave trade, but
their attitude gradually changed during the eighteenth century. At first,
their leaders and assemblies encouraged humane treatment of slaves,
and then they urged members to manumit their slaves. In 1776, the
Friends Yearly Meeting of Philadelphia advocated the excommunica-
tion of members who refused to manumit their slaves. Seven years later,
Quakers petitioned both the British Parliament and the U.S. Congress
to pass laws ending the slave trade. Many Methodists and other evangelicals, including the former slave trader John Newton (1725–1807),
also opposed slavery. In his 1774 pamphlet, *Thoughts on Slavery,*
Methodist founder John Wesley (1703–91) left no doubt about his
opposition to the slave trade:

> I would to God it [the slave trade] may never be found [any] more:
> that we never more steal and sell our brethren like beasts; never
> murder them by thousands. Oh, may this worse than . . . pagan
> abomination be removed from us forever.[6]

The leading abolitionists in England and North America were
motivated by religious as well as humanitarian ideals. One of the early
U.S. advocates for ending the slave trade was Pennsylvania Quaker
Anthony Benezet (1713–84). He studied the evolvement of the slave
trade and wrote a *Historical Account of Guinea,* to illustrate its development as a primary source of African slaves. He also corresponded
actively with abolitionists in England. His writings influenced John
Wesley and British abolitionists Granville Sharp (1735–1813) and
Thomas Clarkson (1760–1846). The latter is best remembered for his
thorough research on the conditions aboard slave ships, which he used
to influence members of Parliament against the slave trade.

Changing Attitudes and Laws

One of the earliest anti-slavery organizations was the Pennsylvania Abolition Society, essentially a Quaker organization, founded in
1775. The anti-slavery movement gained momentum during the next
decade, when the London Abolition Committee was established in

1787, and expanded it into a national crusade in Britain. The next year, the Société des Amis des Noirs (Friends of the Blacks) was founded in France, and in 1789, both the Providence Society for Abolishing the Slave Trade and the Virginia Abolition Society were established.[7] These societies distributed pamphlets and sponsored public meetings and speakers. British abolitionists organized boycotts of slave-produced sugar in order to influence public opinion. These organizations also sponsored mass petition campaigns in hopes of influencing legislative bodies to end the slave trade.

Overall, the abolitionists were quite successful in changing people's attitudes, but passing abolitionist laws was more difficult. West Indian lobbies representing the planters and slave traders were powerful in Britain and France, as was the plantocracy (slave-owning class) in the southern United States. Although abolitionists wanted to end slavery, they initially focused on ending the slave trade, because fewer people had a stake in slave traffic than in the institution of slavery itself. The information Clarkson collected created a very negative image of the slave trade and persuaded many individuals that it should be stopped.

William Wilberforce (1759–1833), a devout evangelical who considered the traffic "the greatest evil," led the battle to end the slave trade in the British Parliament.[8] At just fourteen, he condemned the slave traffic in a letter to a newspaper, and later, when he became a member of the House of Commons in 1780, he repeatedly introduced legislation to end it. In response, Parliament passed the Dolben Act in 1788, designed to improve conditions aboard slave ships. It limited the number of slaves transported to a maximum of five for every three tons, and required that each slave ship have a certified surgeon onboard and commanded by an experienced captain. When the act was renewed in 1799, it put further restrictions on space allowed for slaves.[9]

In 1792, a resolution to abolish the traffic altogether gained a majority in the House of Commons, but the House of Lords vetoed it. Extensive warfare with France during the following years slowed the campaign, but Parliament finally approved the bill to end British participation in the traffic in 1807.

In 1808, the U.S. Congress ended the importation of slaves, in accordance with the provision in the Constitution drafted twenty years earlier. Several states, including Rhode Island, Connecticut, New York,

Massachusetts, and Pennsylvania, had already enacted such limitations in 1787 and 1788. The Danish government ended its participation in the slave trade in 1792–1803 (see "Chronology of Events").

An important challenge to the legality of slavery itself was the Somerset case of 1772. Three years earlier, slave owner Charles Stuart had sailed from Virginia to England accompanied by a slave named James Somerset. In 1771, Somerset escaped, but was apprehended and then put aboard a ship headed for Jamaica, where Stuart planned to sell him. Abolitionists, led by Clarkson, who had often protected runaway slaves, defended Somerset, claiming that slavery was illegal under English law. After a lengthy trial, Chief Justice William Mansfield ruled that English law did not permit Somerset's exportation and sale overseas. Although Mansfield failed to state that slavery was incompatible with English common law, abolitionists and newspapers gave it that interpretation. Actually, slaves remained vulnerable in England until Britain abolished slavery throughout its empire in 1833. Nevertheless, the trial was a victory for both Somerset and the abolition cause.[10]

The Impact of Slave Resistance

A frequently unsung force for abolition was the action of slaves themselves. If Africans resisted their enslavement during the Middle Passage, they were no more willing to submit to bondage after landing in the Americas. Numerous cases of individual defiance, escape, and all-out rebellion mark the history of American slavery. Such acts created fear among slave owners, undermined the system, and strengthened the cause of abolition.

A frequent form of slave protest was to run away, most effective in forested or mountainous areas where fugitives could hide and defend themselves. Communities of runaway slaves date back to the sixteenth century and are generally referred to as maroon societies, as they were known in Jamaica. In Spanish American colonies, such communities were often referred to as *palenques,* and in Brazil as *quilombos.* Recently arrived slaves (*bozals*) were usually more prone to attempt escape than Creoles, who were born in the Americas.[11]

One of the earliest and longest-lasting maroon communities was Palmares, which emerged in the interior of Brazil in the sixteenth century and lasted until 1695. Effective and enduring maroon societies were also established in the tropical rain forests of the Dutch colony of Surinam. These Djuka and Saramaka communities fought off Dutch authorities and negotiated a series of peace treaties during the 1760s, which gave them independence in return for turning over future deserters from the plantations. They were still viable communities when slavery was abolished in the 1860s (see illustration 10).[12]

Full-scale slave rebellions instilled fear and called into question the viability of the oppressive slave system. Nine revolts took place in Bahia, Brazil, between 1807 and 1835. Slaves nearly gained control over the Dutch colony at Berbice, in today's Guyana, in 1762–63. Another widespread revolt took place in nearby Demerara in 1823. In the United States, Nat Turner's revolt in 1831 and foiled plots led by Gabriel Prosser in 1800 and Denmark Vesey in 1822 undermined the slave system.[13]

The most dramatic and successful slave rebellion of all occurred in the French colony of St. Domingue (today's Haiti), on the island of Hispaniola, during the 1790s. By 1802, the slaves had overrun the neighboring Spanish colony of Santa Domingo as well. Their leader, Toussaint L'Ouverture (ca. 1744–1803), won the slaves' freedom, but he was captured and imprisoned in France, where he died in 1803. His successor, Jean-Jacques Dessalines (ca. 1758–1806), renamed the country Haiti in 1804, and it has remained independent.[14]

Diplomatic Efforts to End the Slave Trade

Although Eric Williams argued that Britain no longer needed slavery in the early nineteenth century, and that British abolitionists had merely been advocates of national economic interest, recent studies have demonstrated that the British slave trade and the slave colonies were still prospering. Nevertheless, abolitionists were able to convince much of the British public and a majority of Parliament that free labor was superior to slave labor.[15] Once the slave trade was abolished, British policymakers became committed to entirely ending the Atlantic slave traffic. Many planters in the West were still clamoring for more African slaves, giving nations still involved in the traffic an incentive to import slaves illegally into British colonies, and complicating the implementation of the Act of Abolition.

The issue was not acute in 1808, when Europe was absorbed by the Napoleonic wars and Britain was supreme at sea. Although Britain's

Portuguese allies agreed to curtail their slaving activities, their efforts were ineffectual. When peace returned to Europe in 1815, however, British officials actively pursued every available opportunity to convince other nations to halt the traffic. They persuaded the major continental powers at the Congress of Vienna (1814–15) to condemn the slave trade in principle. France went along reluctantly, and would have resisted if Napoleon had not abolished the traffic during his brief return as emperor in the spring of 1815. Through diplomatic pressure, Britain persuaded the Netherlands to end its involvement in the slave trade, and it forced Portugal and Spain to limit their traffic to African regions south of the equator in 1817. Gradually, Britain created a vast network of treaties with several countries to limit or discontinue the traffic.[16]

British diplomatic efforts also extended to Africa itself. Abolitionists realized that slave merchants in both Africa and Europe needed alternatives to trading in human commodities. At the same time, the Enlightenment roused scientific curiosity, including interest in the geography of Africa's interior. These forces combined to create exploratory expeditions, usually sponsored by private organizations, which sought new discoveries, fresh commercial opportunities, and confronted the slave trade in the African interior.[17] The British negotiated forty-five treaties with West African states between 1840 and 1857, and signed similar treaties with political leaders in the Congo region and subsequently in East Africa. However, African chiefs often disregarded these treaties because they usually gave generous trade advantages to the British and no significant benefits to Africans. But Britain used the treaties to destroy coastal slaving stations and to justify intrusions into African territory. Combating the slave trade and slavery within Africa eventually became a rationale for occupying much of the continent during the second half of the nineteenth century.[18]

Illicit Trade and Its Suppression

Despite Britain's diplomatic efforts, the Atlantic slave trade continued for many decades, illegally from West Africa, and legally from the region south of the equator. Even after the British and American abolition of the trade in 1808, approximately three million Africans were shipped across the Atlantic, nearly a third of the entire traffic. Initially the traffic declined after 1808, but during the 1820s annual shipments rose to sixty thousand, about the same volume as during the last decade before abolition and not far below the 1770s and 1780s peak.[19] France and the United States reluctantly cooperated with British efforts to stop the illicit traffic; their refusal to participate in mutual ship searches may have stemmed from their continued involvement at that time. However, both countries eventually condemned the traffic and joined the British in an anti-slave-trade naval campaign, with the U.S. Congress declaring the slave trade the equivalent of piracy in 1820. Spain and Portugal were more persistent in continuing the traffic, first legally south of the equator, and later in violation of treaty agreements.

In 1819, Britain spearheaded the establishment of an anti-slave-trade squadron, a naval unit that patrolled the West African coast to intercept illegal slave ships. As illustrated by King Osei Bonsu's appeal in 1824 (see document 13), many African merchants and rulers did not want to halt the traffic. A large number of European and American slave merchants also wanted to continue the traffic, but illicit trading posed special problems. To avoid apprehension by authorities, slaves often had to be boarded at night, and capture by the anti-slave-trade squadrons could result in confiscation and prosecution. As more nations joined the effort to end the traffic, illicit traders resorted to ever more evasive maneuvers. Large slave trade firms, on the other hand, adapted to the situation by developing new strategies that resulted in shorter crossings and more children in the transports. After 1850, they used larger and faster vessels, including steam ships, which also tended to reduce slave revolts. For a while, mortality on the Middle Passage remained about the same as in the legal trade, but it increased during the final decades of the illicit traffic. While risks increased, the continuing high demand for slaves made the illicit trade more profitable than the legal traffic had been.[20]

Because Africans rescued by the anti-slave-trade squadrons would most likely have been re-enslaved if returned to their ports of exportation, they were taken to special collection areas on the African coast: Freetown in Sierra Leone by the British, Monrovia in Liberia by the Americans, and Libreville in Gabon by the French. The vast majority of freed slaves were taken to Sierra Leone, among them Samuel Crowther (see "Biographical Sketches"), who later served as a missionary in Nigeria and became the first Anglican bishop in West Africa.

The anti-slave-trade squadrons intercepted approximately one in five illicit slave ships, but only one in sixteen had slaves onboard—the crucial requirement for prosecution. Special "courts of mixed commission" were set up at several places, including Sierra Leone, Havana, Rio de Janeiro, and Paramaribo, to prosecute captured slave traders. These courts were staffed by judges from different countries, including one from the nation of the captured ship, which made it very difficult to obtain a conviction. Furthermore, the actual owner or investor of the apprehended ship was never prosecuted. Only one captain was executed for participating in the slave trade, which was by then considered piracy. Some historians have argued that British naval forces could have completely stopped the slave trade had they put more effort into combating it, but more extreme measures would have violated the national sovereignty of other states, an illegality that discomfited even some abolitionists.[21]

The 160,000 Africans rescued by the squadrons was a small number compared with the three million taken across the Atlantic after 1808. However, as British statesman Viscount Henry Palmerston (1784–1865) noted in assessing the success of suppression efforts:

> To judge the merits of our preventive efforts, we must compare the [number of] slaves now clandestinely carried over . . . with the number that would be so carried if no obstruction were offered to the trade . . . [and] the demand which would have existed if all the Colonies of Great Britain, France, Holland, [and] Denmark had also continued to import annually an unlimited supply of slaves.[22]

Having succeeded in ending British involvement in the Atlantic slave trade, British abolitionists established the London Anti-Slavery Committee in 1823, aimed at abolishing slavery throughout the empire. When this was accomplished between 1834 and 1838, Britain applied pressure on other countries to do the same. It supported the anti-slavery movement in the United States, which culminated in the Civil War and a constitutional amendment abolishing slavery in 1865. By that time, slavery had been abolished in all American countries except in Brazil and the remaining Spanish colonies of Cuba and Puerto Rico. These areas also resisted ending the slave trade, although the latter never developed as a major slave society. The British navy actually attacked slave ships in Brazilian ports in 1850, forcing Brazil to end slave importation or face war with Britain.[23]

Cuba, one of the final vestiges of the huge Spanish American Empire, had developed its slave plantation economy rather late. Its sugar cultivation, patterned on Jamaica's, was stimulated by a temporary British occupation during the 1760s. In the early nineteenth century, Cuba replaced Jamaica and St. Domingue as the largest sugar-producing island in the Caribbean and imported large numbers of slaves. Although the Spanish government had little choice but to submit to British pressure to limit and then end its slave trade in 1817 and 1831 respectively, the treaties had little effect on the slave trade to Cuba because planters there encouraged illegal shipments. Chinese contract laborers arrived in Cuba during the 1850s, but Cuba still imported twelve thousand slaves per year. After 1860, the slave trade dwindled rapidly; the last slave ship from Africa sailed to Cuba in 1867. Three years later, a new law aimed at gradual emancipation granted freedom to slaves over the age of sixty and all children born to slaves. Despite passage of an emancipation law in 1880, a subtle form of slavery survived until Cuba finally abolished slavery in 1886.[24]

The largest importer of African slaves, Brazil gradually loosened its ties with Portugal during the nineteenth century. Between 1807 and 1821, the Portuguese royal family made Rio de Janeiro in Brazil the capital of the empire. When King John VI returned to Lisbon in 1821, he left his son Dom Pedro (1789–1834) as regent of Brazil, but conflict between Brazil and Portugal prompted Brazilian leaders to proclaim Dom Pedro emperor of an independent Brazil in 1822. After 1850, Brazilians had to accept the inevitability of ending slave importation, as well as preparing to abolish slavery. In 1871, Brazil adopted a gradual emancipation law that freed all newborn slave children. A popular abolition movement, on the model of Britain and the United States, started in 1880 and culminated in the abolition of the remaining Brazilian slaves in 1888.[25]

From Slavery to Contract Labor

As the slave trade and chattel slavery were being abolished in the Americas, slaves deserted the West Indian plantations, resulting in a serious decline of the plantation economies. Planters tried to attract workers by other methods, primarily semiservile contract labor from Africa and Asia. Chinese, Indian, and Indonesian workers were enticed to immigrate to American colonies and work at plantations under conditions similar to those of slavery. Africans were also recruited as so-called contract laborers and went to many of the same places where slaves had served before. Ironically, many of the freed slaves at Sierra Leone immigrated to the West Indies, while other slaves freed by the anti-slave-trade squadron remained on the ships and continued the voyage as contract laborers.[26]

Sharecropping became an alternative production method for former slaves in some areas, but often with dubious results. Many of the tropical commodities once grown in the Americas were increasingly cultivated in Africa and Asia, where labor was cheap, while most former slave plantation economies in the West declined. In most areas, where slavery had once been the primary mode of production, various forms of repression and poverty persisted for freed slaves and their descendants.

Notes

1. Seymour Drescher, *From Slavery to Freedom: Comparative Studies in the Rise and Fall of Atlantic Slavery* (New York: New York University Press, 1999), 355–78. See references to Eric Williams in chapter 4.

2. Robert R. Palmer, *The Age of the Democratic Revolution: A Political History of Europe and America, 1760–1800* (Princeton, N.J.: Princeton University Press, 1959–64).

3. David Brion Davis, *The Problem of Slavery in Western Culture* (Ithaca, N.Y.: Cornell University Press, 1966), 42.

4. Jean-Jacques Rousseau, *The Social Contract,* quoted in Roger Anstey, *The Atlantic Slave Trade and British Abolition, 1760–1810* (London: Macmillan, 1975), 120; Davis, *The Problem of Slavery,* 48.

5. Anstey, *The Atlantic Slave Trade and British Abolition,* 126–41.

6. John Wesley, *Thoughts on Slavery,* quoted in Anstey, *The Atlantic Slave Trade and British Abolition,* 240.

7. See the chronology of abolition and emancipation in Davis, *The Problem of Slavery,* 23–36.

8. Anstey, *The Atlantic Slave Trade and British Abolition,* 182. See also 171–72, 250–55, 270–84, 364–402.

9. James A. Rawley, *The Trans-Atlantic Slave Trade: A History* (New York: W. W. Norton, 1981), 258, 293, 303–4.

10. See Davis, *The Problem of Slavery,* 469–501; James Walvin, *Black and White: The Negro in English Society, 1555–1945* (London: Penguin Press, 1973), 117–31.

11. Richard Price, ed., *Maroon Societies: Rebel Slave Communities in the Americas,* 2d ed. (Baltimore, Md.: Johns Hopkins University Press, 1979).

12. Jim Hoogbergen, '*De Bosnegers zijn gekomen!*' *Slavernij en Rebellie in Suriname* (Amsterdam: Promethius, 1992), 7–27.

13. Price, *Maroon Societies,* 171–74; Emelia Viotti da Costa, *Crowns of Glory, Tears of Blood: The Demerara Slave Rebellion of 1823* (New York: Oxford University Press, 1994). Numerous plots and acts of slave rebellion are analyzed in Herbert Aptheker, *American Negro Slave Revolts* (1943; reprint, New York: International Publishers, 1963).

14. David Eltis, *Economic Growth and Ending of the Transatlantic Slave Trade* (Oxford: Oxford University Press, 1987), 209; C. L. R. James, *The Black Jacobins: Toussaint L'Ouverture and the San Domingo Revolution,* 2d ed. revised (1963; New York: Vintage Books, 1989).

15. Eltis, *Economic Growth and Ending of the Transatlantic Slave Trade,* 4. See also chapter 10, "Beyond Economic Interest," in Seymour Drescher, *Econocide: British Slavery in the Era of Abolition* (Pittsburgh, Pa.: University of Pittsburgh Press, 1977); Drescher, *From Slavery to Freedom,* 386–88.

16. For a more detailed description of the British efforts, see Herbert S. Klein, *The Atlantic Slave Trade* (New York: Cambridge University Press, 1999), chapter 8.

17. See Christopher Hibbert, *Africa Explored: Europeans in the Dark Continent, 1769–1889* (New York: Norton, 1982).

18. Suzanne Miers, *Britain and the Ending of the Slave* Trade (New York: Holmes and Meier, 1975). See also Patrick Manning, ed., *Slave Trades, 1500–1800: Globalization of Forced Labor* (Aldershot, U.K.: Ashgate Publishing, 1996), chapter 3.

19. Klein, *The Atlantic Slave Trade,* 193.

20. Eltis, *Economic Growth and Ending of the Transatlantic Slave Trade,* 97–101, 125–37, 145, 161.

21. Eltis, *Economic Growth and Ending of the Transatlantic Slave Trade,* 86; Hugh Thomas, *The Slave Trade: The Story of the Atlantic Slave Trade* (New York: Simon and Schuster, 1997), 774.

22. Quoted in Eltis, *Economic Growth and Ending of the Transatlantic Slave Trade,* 125.

23. Drescher, *From Slavery to Freedom,* 131, 141.

24. Laird W. Bergad, *The Cuban Slave Market, 1790–1880,* Cambridge Latin American Studies 79 (New York: Cambridge University Press, 1995), 23–37; Klein, *The Atlantic Slave Trade,* 192.

25. See Drescher, *From Slavery to Freedom,* 119–57.

26. See Michael Twaddle, ed., *The Wages of Slavery: From Chattel Slavery to Wage Labor in Africa, the Caribbean and England* (London: Frank Cass, 1993); Johnson U. J. Asiegbu, *Slavery and the Politics of Liberation, 1787–1861* (New York: Longman, Green and Co., 1969).

CHAPTER 6

THE LEGACY OF THE ATLANTIC SLAVE TRADE

Transition into Slavery

The journey across the Atlantic to the New World was a horrendous ordeal for enslaved Africans, and the life that awaited them was full of uncertainty. At the end of the voyage were another auction block, physical examinations, and sometimes another branding. Still, the end of the ocean crossing sometimes brought new hope for the slaves. They were on solid ground again; in most instances, fresh food and water were made available, and clothes were issued in preparation for their sale. There are some indications that there was a festive side to the occasion, for which some slaves cut their hair and decorated each other. A contemporary drawing of such an event shows arriving slaves indeed rather relaxed (see illustration 8). The account of Equiano's (see document 12) arrival at Barbados also exhibits a sense of relief, although it was soon shattered by their sale and the separation of friends and loved ones. Occasionally, shipmates ended up at the same plantation, or near enough that they could continue their association. The strong bonds that had developed between them during the Middle Passage caused them to feel like family, as brothers and sisters, and their children would refer to other shipmates as aunt or uncle.[1]

Most new arrivals entered their new communities at the bottom of the social stratum, the lowest among the slaves. Indications are that the slave community welcomed them, but their introduction to the hard labor would undoubtedly be a shock. The experiences varied from place to place, but adjustment to a new location and a new life must have been very difficult for the arriving slaves. If they ended up at a plantation or other crowded workplace, they might meet other slaves who spoke their language, rediscover a relative or an acquaintance, or keep alive a friendship made on the voyage. Their memories of Africa and their journey would contribute to the new culture they would create in their new world.

The Demographic and Economic Impact

With the transportation of nearly ten million Africans across the Atlantic, it was inevitable that they should become a significant portion of American populations and have an important influence on the cultures that developed there. By 1850, African Americans constituted about 20 percent of the New World population, a significant number in itself. Their economic contribution was far greater than their numbers between 1600 and 1800, however, because most worked at plantations that produced tropical commodities for which there was a growing demand in the world markets. According to Robert Fogel:

> Sugar was the single most important of the internationally traded commodities, dwarfing the value of trade in grain, meat, fish, tobacco, cattle, spices, cloth, and metals. Shortly before the American Revolution sugar by itself accounted for about a fifth of all English imports and with the addition of tobacco, coffee, cotton, and rum, the share of slave-produced commodities in England's imports was about 30 percent . . . It was not just Britain but also France, Spain, Portugal, Holland, and Denmark that thrived on buying from or selling to slave colonies.[2]

The largest influx of slaves and the highest mortality rates were in tropical colonies of the Caribbean islands and Guiana, where sugar was the main crop. As a result of continual importation, the majority of the slaves in these areas continued to be African-born until the slave trade ended. The distribution of Africans in the Americas was also rather uneven. In some Caribbean islands and the Guianas, Blacks comprised 90 percent of the population. In Brazil, which received nearly four million slaves or 41 percent of the entire Atlantic traffic, slaves were about a third of the population by the 1820s, and freed mulattos and Blacks constituted an additional third. People of African or part-African descent were perhaps more than half of the population in Venezuela by 1800, but less than 20 percent in Mexico. The African American population in Peru and Argentina was about 30 and 25 percent respectively by the end of the eighteenth century. In most northern U.S. states and Canada, on the other hand, African Americans constituted less than 2 percent.[3]

Mortality rates were considerably lower and birthrates much higher in the United States than in tropical colonies, resulting in high natural increase in its Black population, despite relatively late and modest importation of slaves. In 1680, there were fewer than seven thousand slaves in the North American mainland colonies, and in the 1730s there were 120,000, less than 5 percent of the population. By 1770, however, they increased to 22 percent. Although fewer than 400,000 slaves were brought to the U.S. territory—less than 4 percent of the total Atlantic traffic (see table 3.3)—by 1825 there were about 1,750,000 slaves. This was more than one-third of all the slaves in the Americas at that time, and more than 80 percent of them had been born in America.[4]

In the United States, slaves were initially concentrated in the Carolinas and Georgia and were employed in general farming, as well as tobacco, rice, and indigo cultivation. After the invention of the cotton gin in 1793, cotton agriculture boosted slaveholding tremendously and spread slavery west of the Mississippi. As the country's economy became increasingly based on cotton agriculture and the textile industry, abolitionist sentiment prevalent during the revolutionary era waned.

The situation in the British West Indies was quite different. After slavery was abolished during the 1830s, most liberated slaves deserted the plantations and caused a serious decline of the plantation economies. Planters tried to replace the workers with semiservile contract laborers from Africa and Asia or immigrants from Europe, but they failed to revive production. A few decades later, the same process took place in the Caribbean colonies of other European nations. Consequently, many European planters and their assistants returned to Europe, which raised the percentages of the Black populations in the Caribbean. However, a subsequent wave of Asian immigrants lowered the percentages again.

Slave Communities and Cultural Influences

Though exploited and placed in subservient positions, slaves were amazingly resilient. Robbed of their family connections, they created communities and subcultures that preserved many elements of their ancestral African cultures. Ethnic ties and ancestral languages often provided the foundation for the new communities, but mixed with elements of the dominant culture in which the slaves lived. Preserving African cultural elements was easier at plantations and in towns, where slaves might find people with similar cultural values, languages, and religious beliefs. Recent research suggests that slave traders incidentally aided this process by obtaining slaves from the same African region on successive voyages and shipping them to the same destinations. Thus, people of a particular ethnic background often ended up in the same area of the New World.[5]

It is difficult for languages to withstand the process of cultural assimilation, especially in bilingual relationships (when partners speak different languages) or when the language of the master had to be used regularly. Slaves often developed a so-called pidgin language, which consisted of a small, mixed vocabulary without much attention to grammatical correctness. Gradually, pidgin evolved into creole languages such as Sranan in Surinam and Papiamento in the lower Caribbean. More African elements survived in long-lasting maroon communities such as the Saramaka and Ndjuka languages in the Surinam interior (see illustration 10). In most places, however, only minor remnants of African languages remained after several generations.[6]

No uniform African American culture could develop in the Americas because African slaves came from a myriad of different cultures and ethnic groups and were distributed across a wide variety of national and cultural entities. Locally, slaves were often able to establish subcultures within the dominant culture, particularly on large plantations where they lived village-style in separate quarters from the owners and managers. Despite many obstacles, slaves usually maintained contact with neighboring communities, and those on small plantations or farms had to rely even more on such contacts.

It appears that the family played a more important role in slave life than has often been thought. Family and community activities were crucial in perpetuating traditions and values through stories, music, celebrations, and religious gatherings. Most slaves found comfort in Christianity, which they adapted to their own situation and found a powerful spiritual identification with Jesus the Savior and Moses the Deliverer, who they believed understood their pain and suffering. Their so-called Negro Spirituals frequently alluded to suffering and injustice, from which they wished to escape. Despite forced behavior to the contrary, most slaves never accepted the inferior status imposed on them, and in their religious gatherings they often found relief, believing that God was on their side.[7]

Nevertheless, African culture has greatly influenced American and world cultures. The African influence on music is most evident in jazz, rock, and other types of music where rhythm is important, and "Negro Spirituals" and gospel music have spread throughout the Christian world. The use of specific tools, dances, and dress patterns, as well as food preparation, basket making, and many other practices have African roots. Although they may not be traceable to a specific region, African designs are clearly evident in pottery making. Many religious beliefs and practices, from honoring ancestors to particular ceremonies, also exhibit African origins.[8]

While slave owners wielded enormous power, they often allowed their slaves some elements of freedom and self-expression. The owners were, after all, in the business to benefit economically from the labor of slaves, and they used a variety of measures to achieve their goals, including punishment and reward. Slaves possessed their own methods of cooperation and obstruction, and they developed subtle techniques to gain concessions. In the West Indies and the United States, slaves sometimes had their own plot of land, which they worked during the weekends or on holidays to accumulate wealth that might ultimately enable them to secure their freedom, although such options were more limited in the United States.

New World Slavery and Racism

New World slavery exhibited some characteristics not found in earlier systems. One of these was the use of large plantations, initially developed for sugar cultivation, that required large numbers of slaves organized in a highly disciplined labor regimen not unlike the factory system that started in eighteenth-century Britain. American plantation slavery developed a highly structured gang system, and slaves resented the monotonous work and long hours, just as factory workers did. Slaves, however, had few opportunities to escape the system, and punishment could be severe if they tried. While average working hours may have been longer in the early factories than on the plantations, factory

workers could quit, although they and their families might face starva-
tion. Slaves, on the other hand, did not even have that option.[9]

Another disturbing feature of New World slavery was its basis in
race. From the beginning of regular contact with Africans, Europeans saw
themselves and their culture as superior, but they also felt superior to
other non-Europeans, as well as to their European neighbors. Such attitudes tend to be universal, but as Europeans enslaved Africans in increasing numbers and enslavement of Europeans diminished, the words
African and *slave* became increasingly synonymous in their minds. This
attitude was even more evident among Europeans living in American
slave societies. Racist attitudes also appeared to be stronger among
Anglo-Saxons than among their Latin counterparts. Comparing racial
attitudes between Brazil and the United States, Carl Degler claimed, "in
Brazil the slave may have been feared, but the black man was not,
whereas in the United States both the slave and the black were feared."[10]

Racism, or stereotyping persons on the basis of their physical
appearance such as skin color, hair texture, and the like, became a persistent consequence of New World slavery. Even after slavery was abolished, racism remained a major social problem for descendants of slaves
in most American societies. Ironically, just as slavery and the slave trade
were being abolished, many scientists and social scientists began offer-
ing "evidence" for race-based characteristics and qualities. This so-
called scientific racism was popularized during the late nineteenth and
early twentieth century, and Nazi racism of the 1930s and 1940s was a
belated manifestation of it. By that time, however, the scientific community had decidedly rejected such notions.

It is not uncommon for people to compare the slave trade and
slavery with the Nazi Holocaust, because racism, high mortality rates,
and deprivation of freedom were common in both. That comparison,
however, is problematic. The object of the Holocaust was to kill Jews,
while slave traders wanted to disembark as many African slaves as possible and land them at their American destination in good condition,
and slaveholders wanted to keep them alive as workers.[11]

The Historical Perspective

The Atlantic slave trade is one of the most tragic chapters in human
history. It lasted nearly four centuries and involved millions of innocent

people who were torn from their families and shipped to a place from which only a few would ever return. They were forced into a system of slavery that bound them for life and their descendants after them. When slavery was abolished, most of the former slaves and their offspring were relegated to second-class citizenship and often faced the humiliation of racial prejudice. Historian Henry Louis Gates believes that:

> Until we as a society fully reckon with the history of slavery in all its dimensions . . . and overcome our historical denial of the central shaping role that slavery has played in the creation of all America's social, political, cultural, and economic institutions, we cannot truly begin to confront the so-called race problem in this country.[12]

Examining the roots of slavery is a challenge that many historians have applauded. Since the international civil rights movement after the Second World War, and particularly after the 1960s, many historians have devoted time and energy to gain a better understanding of slavery and the slave trade. Numerous studies have been published on the subject, and that trend is still continuing.

In studying any historical topic, the historian must recognize that earlier generations had different standards and values than the present one, just as different societies often have different standards of right and wrong. In a sense, the past is like a foreign country. For example, the concepts of individual liberty and equality have had different meanings at different times. Before the Enlightenment in the late eighteenth century, these concepts applied only to specific groups of people. Aristocrats or noblemen could carry swords or wear fur, while the lower classes could not. The testimony of a middle-class businessman carried far more weight in court than that of a peasant, one who merely worked the land. People knew their place, or were supposed to. Women were generally barred from owning property in their own name, and could not vote where men of the same standing could. The first stirring slogans of equality and liberty of the democratic revolutions did not necessarily apply to slaves, women, or peasants. This is still true today in many of the world's societies. For these reasons, historian David Eltis cautions that scholars should try to understand the culture they study:

> We have more than enough evidence to condemn what happened in the past. . . . Yet if condemn on the basis of modern values is all we do, then we are never likely to understand the past. At the very

least, condemnation of wrong thinking in earlier societies should emerge from circumspect reflection on how present attitudes will appear to posterity.[13]

Placed in the broad picture of human history, the Atlantic slave trade has left a profound legacy in its impact on the Atlantic community or civilization that is still evolving. As people moved from Europe and Africa to the Americas, they not only spread plants, animals, and diseases throughout the territories around the Atlantic, but also commingled with each other and integrated economic practices, artistic patterns, cultural norms, and a variety of concepts. This convergence of different peoples and cultures may initially have created tensions that led to exploitation of the weaker by the more aggressive, but from the process of interaction emerged new ideas, practices, and opportunities. Historians are increasingly recognizing the development of a common culture among the people living on the continents bordering the Atlantic. Instead of a barrier, the ocean acted as a conduit that brought about an intermingling of people and merged ways of life, predominantly European, but also African and American.[14] Ironically, the slave trade played a decisive role in making Africa, its people, and its cultures a part of that common legacy. Without it, American societies would be much different than they are today.

For the Africans who were forced to cross the Atlantic, a positive influence would have been impossible to imagine. Their plight is almost inconceivable from the perspective of our time and the privileges enjoyed by most people in modern societies. The past and the present are both linked and yet so distant. We cannot change the past, but we must try to understand it if we are to be enlightened by it. The American philosopher Santayana once suggested, "those who forget the past are condemned to repeat it." Knowledge of history has the potential to instill greater understanding, compassion, and wisdom.

Slavery and similar forms of exploitation still exist in some societies, such as in the Sudan in northeastern Africa. Let us hope that the lessons learned from studying the Atlantic slave trade will ensure that these practices will be ended and that such an assault on human freedom and dignity will never happen again.

Notes

1. See Sidney Mintz and Richard Price, *The Birth of African-American Culture* (Boston, Mass.: Beacon Press, 1976), 42–43.

2. Robert W. Fogel, *Without Consent or Contract: The Rise and Fall of American Slavery* (New York: Norton, 1989), 21–22.

3. James Lockhart and Stuart B. Schwartz, *Early Latin America: A History of Colonial Spanish America and Brazil* (New York: Cambridge University Press, 1983), 342–43, 383, 401.

4. Fogel, *Without Consent or Contract,* 29–34. See also table 3.3, which contains the most recent arrival statistics.

5. David Geggus, "The French Slave Trade: An Overview," *William and Mary Quarterly* 58 (January 2001): 133–34.

6. John Thornton, *Africa and Africans in the Making of the Atlantic World, 1400–1800,* 2d ed. (1992; New York: Cambridge University Press, 1998), 212–18; Richard Price, *The Guiana Maroons; A Historical and Biographical Introduction* (Baltimore, Md.: Johns Hopkins University Press, 1976), 20, 60–62.

7. See chapter 6, "Changing Interpretations of Slave Culture," in Robert W. Fogel, *Without Consent or Contract,* 154–98.

8. See Thornton, *Africa and Africans in the Making of the Atlantic World,* 317–34.

9. Fogel, *Without Consent or Contract,* 21–29, 395.

10. Carl N. Degler, *Neither Black nor White: Slavery and Race Relations in Brazil and the United States* (New York: MacMillan, 1971), 89.

11. Seymour Drescher, *From Slavery to Freedom: Comparative Studies in the Rise and Fall of Atlantic Slavery* (New York: New York University Press, 1999), 275–332.

12. See "Preface" in *William and Mary Quarterly* 58 (January 2001): 5.

13. David Eltis, *The Rise of African Slavery in the Americas* (New York: Cambridge University Press, 2000), xiii.

14. See chapter 1, "Birth of an Atlantic World," in Thornton, *Africa and Africans in the Making of the Atlantic World.*

Slave coffle, marching in chain-gang style to the East African Coast. Reproduced with permission from the Collections of the Library of Congress.

Branding of slaves after being sold to Europeans. Reprinted with permission of Corbis-Bettmann, New York.

Slaves ferried in canoes to the slave ship. Reproduced with permission of the Hakluyt Society.

View of the trading castle at Elmina, Gold Coast (Ghana). Reproduced with permission from the Collections of the Library of Congress.

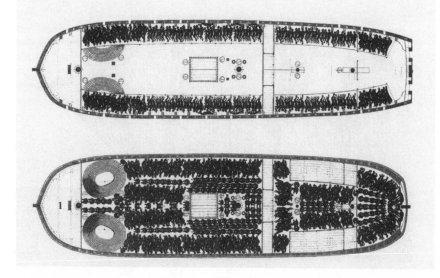

Slave quarters between decks aboard the slave ship *L'Aurore*. Reproduced with permission of Archéologie Navale Classique Recherche Édition (ANCRE).

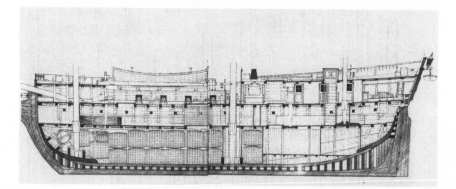

Decks and storage areas of the slave ship *L'Aurore*. Reproduced with permission of Archéologie Navale Classique Recherche Édition (ANCRE).

Slave ships off the coast of St. Eustatius. Reproduced with permission of Sticht-ing Atlas Van Stolk, Rotterdam.

Group of Negroes, as imported to be sold for Slaves.

Slaves arriving in Surinam. Reproduced with permission from Richard Price and Sally Price, eds., *Stedman's Surinam: Life in an Eighteenth-Century Slave Society*, Baltimore: Johns Hopkins University Press, 1992.

Newly arrived African slaves for sale in Brazil. Reproduced with permission of the Cornell University Library, Division of Rare and Manuscript Collections.

A Rebel Negro armed & on his guard.

A maroon in the Surinam hinterland. Reproduced with permission from Richard Price and Sally Price, eds., *Stedman's Surinam: Life in an Eighteenth-Century Slave Society,* Baltimore: Johns Hopkins University Press, 1992.

BIOGRAPHICAL SKETCHES:
SIGNIFICANT PERSONS IN THE ATLANTIC SLAVE TRADE

Bartolomé de Las Casas (1474–1566)

Bartolomé de Las Casas is perhaps best remembered for his suggestion that Africans be brought to the New World to supply the labor needed. The proposal came in his 1552 book, *The Devastation of the Indies,* an appeal for intervention from political and religious authorities in Europe to protect American Indians from the inhumane exploits of the Spanish conquistadors and colonists. He later came to regret, and retracted, the proposition.

Las Casas was born in Seville, Spain, in 1474, to a family of merchants who had close links with Spanish expansion into the Americas; his father and three uncles had sailed on Columbus's second voyage to the New World. Because the family was wealthy, Bartolomé could study instead of going into business and was drawn to the classics. In 1502, he went to America as an adventurer, but five years later, he traveled to Rome to be ordained a deacon. Returning to Hispaniola, he became the first priest ordained in the Americas in 1512.

The cruelty dealt Amerindians through conquest and forced labor in mining and agriculture bothered the young priest. He advocated their peaceful conversion and inclusion in the Christian community, instead of exploitation in the *encomienda,* the system of forced labor. He preached against their brutal treatment at the hands of the Spanish, but his criticism offended the Spanish colonists, who complained to authorities in Spain and Rome. Las Casas had to defend his views to royal and papal representatives.

While he failed to change the behavior of Spanish colonists in 1537, he received moral support from the papal encyclical *Sublimis*

Deus, which proclaimed that American Indians were rational beings with souls. The Spanish emperor Charles V allowed Las Casas to establish missions in Guatemala, and in 1542, the Crown declared Indian slavery illegal. In 1544, Las Casas was appointed bishop of Chiapas, Mexico, but because he insisted that Spaniards obey the law of 1542 and free their slaves or be denied communion, his life was threatened. Recalled to Spain in 1547, he was invited by the emperor to debate his views regarding Amerindians with a scholarly opponent.

Las Casas resigned his bishopric in 1550, withdrew to a monastery, and devoted himself to writing. He published his *Devastation of the Indies* without approval from the Spanish Inquisition, the religious authority charged with protecting official doctrine, but he escaped punishment because of his extraordinary prestige. He continued to write and defend Amerindian rights until his death in 1566.

Ayuba Suleiman Diallo, aka Job ben Solomon (ca. 1700–73)

Born about 1700 in the country of Bondu, between the Senegal and Faleme Rivers in today's Mali, West Africa, Ayuba Suleiman Diallo was a well-educated Muslim merchant whose father and grandfather held prominent political and religious positions in their country. After selling two slaves to a British captain on the Gambia River in 1730, Ayuba and two servants were captured as they returned home and were then sold to the very captain with whom he had earlier traded (see document 4). Shipped to Annapolis, Maryland, he was a slave on a tobacco plantation for two years before Thomas Bluett saw him and recognized that he was no ordinary slave, but a well-educated man. Bluett took him to Britain and published an account of his enslavement, calling him the son of the "High Priest of Boonda." Ayuba became the object of much interest and curiosity and was introduced to prominent members of society, including members of the royal family. Wealthy friends purchased his freedom and arranged with the Royal African Company for his return to Africa. Accompanied by Bluett, Ayuba returned to the Gambia in 1734, but regional warfare prevented travel into the interior for two years. He was reunited with his family in 1736, and two years later, his servant and interpreter who had been enslaved with him was also returned to Africa. He lived until 1773, but there is no record of his final years.

Olaudah Equiano, aka Gustavus Vassa (ca. 1745–97)

Born around 1745 in what is now southeastern Nigeria, Olaudah Equiano was kidnapped by local slave raiders when he was ten or eleven years old, carried to the coast, and sold to slavers bound for the West Indies. Shipped first to Barbados and then to Virginia, he was purchased by a planter and worked on a plantation for three months before being sold to a British naval officer (see document 12). First called Michael, then Jacob, he was given the name Gustavus Vassa by his new master, and he used that name for most of his life. Only after he wrote his memoirs did he use his African name, and then sparingly.

Equiano traveled widely with his new owner and served with him in several military campaigns. Under his tutelage, Equiano learned the English language and became a competent seaman. Despite a promise of freedom, he was returned to the West Indies in 1762 and was resold to a Philadelphia merchant, Richard King. Again put to work at sea, Equiano served as assistant to the captain on one of King's ships. Since King was a Quaker under much pressure to end his complicity in slavery, he allowed Equiano to engage in petty trade on his own, through which he earned enough money to buy his freedom in 1766, at the age of twenty-one.

After his release from slavery, Equiano made his home in Britain. Still much interested in the sea, he toured the Mediterranean and participated in an expedition to the Arctic in search of a northwest passage. In 1787, he served as commissary of stores for the first settlement of freed slaves in Sierra Leone. Dismissed from that post after one year, he returned to Britain and resumed his connection with the abolition movement. Earlier, in 1783, he had brought to the attention of Granville Sharp an incident in which the majority of slaves on the ship *Zong* had been thrown overboard. This information led to one of many parliamentary battles over the slave trade. Urged by abolitionist friends to tell of his experiences with slavery, he wrote *The Interesting Narrative of Olaudah Equiano, or Gustavus Vassa, the African* in 1789, when the debate over the slave trade was raging through Britain. His simple but moving description of his capture (see document 1), experiences as a slave, and achievement as a free man arrested public attention. An instant best-seller, the book became an important contribution to the anti-slavery campaign. Some scholars have questioned Equiano's authorship of the *Narrative*.

Equiano traveled through Britain speaking against the slave trade and selling his book. He married a British woman in 1792 and had one daughter, who died only a few months after him. Equiano died on April 30, 1797, but his book, which went through many editions in Britain, America, Holland, and Germany, continued to rouse opposition to slavery and the slave trade long after his death.

Essjerrie Ettin (ca. 1740–69)

One of very few Africans whose name survives in archival records of the Middle Passage, Essjerrie Ettin was an Asante from the interior of what is today Ghana. All that is known about his short life is that he led a slave revolt on the Dutch slave ship *Guineese Vriendschap* on October 31, 1769, and was executed a month later.

With 358 enslaved Africans onboard, the *Guineese Vriendschap* was ready to begin its voyage across the Atlantic when the slaves rose and almost took control of the ship. They had cut the anchor and set the ship adrift when the warship *Castor* sent two boats of sailors to suppress the uprising. In a futile burst for freedom, several slaves jumped overboard. Four drowned while the others were recaptured, and in the skirmish onboard, one slave was killed and several wounded. Some slaves tried to commit suicide, but were stopped by the crew.

Ten slaves suspected of having led the revolt were brought before the governing council at Elmina, whose director general questioned three of them, presumably including Ettin, who was thought to be the chief leader. Judgment was passed on November 2, 1769, and Ettin was condemned to death. To serve as a deterrent against future revolts, he was executed aboard the *Guineese Vriendschap* in view of the surviving slaves. There is no account of the execution, but according to the sentence, Ettin was to have his right hand severed (his left arm had already been maimed during battle) and then be hung from the ship's mast, his body abused and broken by the crew until he died, and then thrown into the ocean.

James Somerset (ca. 1740s–unknown)

Although little is known about the life of James Somerset, his name appeared regularly in British newspapers in 1772, and he came to symbolize the abolition struggle that captivated the British public during the late eighteenth and early nineteenth centuries.

In 1769, Somerset accompanied his master, Charles Stewart, a Boston customs official, to London for an extended business stay. In 1771, he ran away, but was apprehended and returned to his master. Stewart had his slave imprisoned on a ship bound for Jamaica, where he was to be sold. Before the ship set sail, however, Somerset's plight came to the attention of Granville Sharp (1735–1813), one of Britain's leading abolitionists, who had previously aided several runaways with medical care and legal defense. Sharp immediately obtained a writ of *habeus corpus,* securing Somerset's release and demanding a trial, which was set for early 1772. With Somerset in his custody, Sharp introduced him to many influential people and generated much interest in his fate. His trial started in February and lasted six months. The presiding judge, Lord Chief Justice William Mansfield, had a difficult time coming to a decision and granted several lengthy adjournments—one lasted three months—because the laws concerning slavery in Britain were at that time quite confusing and contradictory. While on the one hand, the enslavement of English subjects had been outlawed, African slaves were regarded as property, and the British forcefully protected property rights.

Final judgment came on June 22, 1772. Somerset was freed on the basis that the law did not permit a person from a foreign country to be forcefully exported from Britain for the purpose of being sold overseas. Newspapers and people sympathetic to the abolition cause hailed the decision as a victory, and interpreted it as meaning anyone entering Britain would legally be a free person. Many historians have perpetuated this interpretation, but while the decision did free Somerset, several runaways were subsequently recaptured in Britain, and some were shipped to the West Indies. Legal cases involving slavery continued to come before the courts, but escaped slaves were not secure in Britain until 1833, when slavery was abolished throughout the British Empire by an act of Parliament.

Phillis Wheatley (ca. 1753–84)

Kidnapped from the Senegal-Gambia region of Africa and shipped to Massachusetts when she was about seven years old, Phillis Wheatley defied all expectations of her race, status, and gender to become an acclaimed poet. Landed in Boston on July 11, 1761, and dressed in rags, she was purchased at auction by merchant John Wheatley as an attendant for his wife. The little girl exhibited an amazing aptitude for learning, which the Wheatleys encouraged, and within sixteen months of her arrival she was reading passages from the Bible and Greek and Latin classics.

Tutored by the Wheatley daughter in English language and literature, religion, Latin, history, geography, and astronomy, Phillis received a thorough education that surpassed what was given to most women of her day. Exhibiting rare talent, she published her first poem at the age of fourteen, in December 1767. Three years later, she caused a sensation in Boston with her elegy "On the Death of the Rev. George Whitefield," about the well-known British evangelical preacher, which was printed in broadside form. Nevertheless, the Wheatleys could not find a Boston printer willing to publish a book of thirty-nine of her poems. In May 1773, they sent her to London, accompanied by their son, where her *Poems on Various Subjects, Religious and Moral* was published later that year. It was the first book of poetry, and probably the first book of any kind, published by an African American.

Although it appears that John Wheatley gave Phillis her freedom after her return from Britain, she continued living with the family and fled with them to Rhode Island when Boston was occupied during the Revolutionary War. A highly acclaimed poem written there to George Washington, then commander of the Continental army, was just one of her many poems published in newspapers and magazines. In 1778, after the deaths of Suzanna and John Wheatley, Phillis married John Peters, a free Black man, whose small grocery store proved inadequate to support them and their three children. Although she continued writing, she could not find a publisher for her work and died in poverty in 1784 at the age of thirty-one. American abolitionists reprinted her poetry in the 1830s as a testimony to the ability of Africans and the triumph of human capacities over circumstances of birth.

Anthony Benezet (1713–84)

Anthony Benezet was one of the early and very influential North American abolitionists. He was born in France in 1713, but his Protestant family moved to Britain to avoid religious persecution. Benezet immigrated to Pennsylvania at the age of eighteen and became a devout member of the Society of Friends, also known as Quakers. Teaching at the Quaker school in Philadelphia, he held classes for children of free

Blacks in the evening. In 1773, he organized a school for Black children, admitting slave children when space was available.

Benezet and his friend John Woolman (1720–72) of New Jersey urged their fellow Friends to manumit, or free their slaves, and were among the first White Americans to advocate the abolition of slavery. In 1775, Benezet helped organize the Pennsylvania Abolition Society, perhaps the first anti-slavery organization in North America, if not the world.

Among Benezet's many correspondents were Benjamin Franklin (1706–90) and John Wesley (1703–91), and British abolitionists Thomas Clarkson (1760–1846) and Granville Sharp (1735–1813). One of the best-informed Americans about Africa in his time, he wrote several pamphlets and books concerning the slave trade and its abolition, including *Some Historical Account of Guinea* (1771). This book greatly influenced John Wesley, who borrowed from it in writing his pamphlet *Thoughts on Slavery*.

Deeply concerned about the welfare of Africans and especially those who were enslaved, Benezet was beloved by Philadelphia's Black community, and when he died in 1784, hundreds of African Americans attended his funeral.

Ignatius Sancho (1729–80)

The most celebrated Afro-Briton before the twentieth century, Ignatius Sancho was born on a slave ship en route to the West Indies in 1729. He spent only two years in the New World, however. After his mother died and his father committed suicide rather than live as a slave, his master took the orphaned two-year-old from the Spanish colony of New Granada (present-day Colombia, Panama, Venezuela, and Ecuador) and presented him as a gift to three unmarried sisters living in Greenwich, England. It was they who gave him the surname Sancho, after the comical squire in *Don Quixote*.

Although the sisters refused to educate him, the boy attracted the interest of a neighbor, the duke of Montague, who gave him books and encouraged his reading. When the duke died in 1749, the twenty-year-old Sancho fled from his owners, sought protection in the home of the duke's widow, and became her butler. When she died two years later, she bequeathed her servant, according to custom among the British nobility, a year's salary and an annual annuity.

Exposed only to the life of Britain's social elites, Sancho tried to find employment as an actor, playing Shakespeare's Black characters, but a speech impediment doomed that effort. In 1766, he became the valet of the late duke's son-in-law, the new duke of Montague. As his personal attendant, Sancho accompanied the duke to all public events, enjoyed a rich social life, and met countless people of wealth and influence. When illness and obesity rendered him unable to continue as valet in 1773, the duke helped him establish a grocery store to support himself and his family. Married in 1758, he and his wife had seven children.

Having had access to a wide variety of books in the Montague household, the self-taught Sancho had developed a broad knowledge of literature and started writing himself. Although he also produced several musical compositions and plays, it was his correspondence with a wide circle of British notables—written in an age when letter writing was an art form on a par with writing poetry—that made him a popular literary figure and challenged the prevailing belief that Africans had inferior intellects. Sancho never enjoyed fame and fortune from his letters, though, for they were collected and published in 1782, two years after his death.

Quobna Ottobah Cugoano (1757–ca. 1801)

Ottobah Cugoano's *Thoughts and Sentiments on the Evil Wicked Traffic of Slavery and Commerce in the Human Species,* published in 1787, was one of the earliest books written by an African for a European audience. He was born to a prominent family in the Fante region of southern Ghana in 1757. When he was about thirteen, he visited an uncle some distance from his family and, while playing in the woods with other children, was kidnapped by slave catchers. The children were forced to walk several days to the slave market at Cape Coast Castle near Accra. Sold to European traders, Cugoano spent only three days in confinement before being herded onto a ship bound for the Caribbean island of Grenada.

Cugoano said the experience of enslavement and transportation was so terrible that during the eight to nine months between his capture and arrival in Grenada he often wished for death. During the voyage, he and other enslaved boys and women, who had more freedom than the men chained below deck, plotted to set the ship afire so that all aboard would perish. Their plan failed when one of the women informed a crew member with whom she had sexual relations.

After working as a slave in Grenada for two years, Cugoano was sold to an Englishman who took him to Britain as his servant. Arriving in Britain in 1772, shortly after the Somerset decision, Cugoano's new master manumitted him, encouraged him to learn to read and write, and advised him to be baptized to guarantee his freedom. He took the Christian name John Stewart, but continued to be identified primarily as Ottobah Cugoano.

Like his African friend, Equiano (see previous biography), Cugoano worked with abolitionists to establish a colony for freed Blacks at Sierra Leone. He had serious reservations about the experiment, however, which were vindicated when high mortality rates and administrative instability plagued the early years of the venture. In 1787, the same year that Sierra Leone was founded, Cugoano published his attack on the slave trade. Although he charged that every Englishman shared responsibility for the slave trade, his book helped to advance the cause of abolition. Cugoano wanted to establish a school for Black children in London, but that was not accomplished until 1807, after his death. He lived with the poor Black community in London, where he died in obscurity in or about 1801.

John Newton (1725–1807)

Born in London in 1725, John Newton participated in the slave trade as a young man but later became an Anglican minister and ardent abolitionist. He is best remembered, however, as author of the hymn "Amazing Grace." His mother died when he was only six years old, and he began his maritime career five years later, going to sea with his father, the captain of a merchant ship. By the time his father retired, young Newton had made six ocean voyages and decided to follow in his father's footsteps. However, being what he described as a rebellious and irresponsible boy, he lost that opportunity when he reported for duty after his ship had already set sail. Impressed into the British navy shortly thereafter, at the age of nineteen, he deserted but was recaptured, publicly flogged, and demoted from midshipman to common seaman.

Transferred to a slave ship, he became the servant to a slave trader operating on the Guinea Coast of Africa. Brutally abused by his master, he said he was, "in effect though not in name," a slave. His father persuaded a friend, another sea captain trading with Africa, to rescue his son and bring him back to Britain. During the return voyage in 1848, the ship nearly sank in a violent storm. Newton called on God's help and, when the ship survived the storm, believed that prayer had spared him. He experienced the incident as a dramatic religious conversion.

Signing on as mate (captain's assistant) on a slave ship and then becoming commander of a ship that made three slaving voyages to Africa, Newton saw no conflict between his new-found religion and his profession. The slave trade was then considered legitimate business, and while Newton found it distasteful, he believed God had placed him there. During these voyages, he studied Latin, read religious books, and conducted devotional services for his crew.

While preparing for his fourth slaving voyage in 1754, he experienced an epileptic seizure that prodded him to give up seafaring and stay with his wife, Mary Catlett, whom he had married four years earlier. At Liverpool, where he served as surveyor of tides for five years, he became a disciple of evangelistic preacher George Whitefield and an admirer of John Wesley, founder of the Methodist Church. Deciding to become a minister himself, he studied on his own and, after much perseverance, was ordained in 1764.

Called to the pastorate of the church at Olney, a small market town in Buckinghamshire, Newton developed into an effective and popular preacher. At the request of a friend, he wrote a series of letters describing his dramatic conversion, which were expanded and collected into a book. Published the same year he began his pastorate at Olney, the book went through several editions in Britain and America and made him a major figure in the growing evangelical movement on both sides of the Atlantic. One of his parishioners, the poet William Cowper, helped him write hymns, and they collaborated on a book of *Olney Hymns,* published in 1779. The next year, he took a more prestigious position as rector of St. Mary Woolnoth in London, where he drew large crowds and became one of the leading ministers of the Church of England during the eighteenth-century evangelical revival. An ardent critic of the slave trade, he published his influential *Thoughts upon the African Slave Trade* in 1788 (see document 7) and became an advisor to leaders of the abolitionist movement. He died in London in 1807.

Toussaint L'Ouverture (ca. 1744–1803)

Born to slavery on the island of Hispaniola, Toussaint L'Ouverture is regarded as the founding father of the country later established on that island—Haiti. The son of an African transported to the West Indies after being taken as a prisoner of war, Toussaint Bréda was born about 1744 in the French colony of St. Domingue. Intelligent and ambitious, he made good use of opportunities for self-education, learned to read and write, and was entrusted with considerable responsibility, which led to his manumission in 1791.

Shortly after gaining his own freedom, Toussaint joined the uprising of St. Domingue's slaves that launched a decade-long struggle for freedom. A genius at organization and tactics, he quickly became the leader of the rebellion and became known as L'Ouverture, meaning "the Opening," in recognition of his valor in creating a gap in the ranks of the enemy. In 1794, France's revolutionary government abolished slavery and subsequently appointed Toussaint governor-general of the island. He drove occupying British forces from the western coast of the island and put down an attempted coup by mulatto generals.

After gaining control over virtually all of Hispaniola by 1801, Toussaint reorganized the government, established a constitution, and began instituting public improvements. However, after Napoleon declared himself emperor in 1802, he rescinded abolition and sent a large military force to reestablish French control of the colony. Plagued by disease and unable to defeat Toussaint's forces, the French had to negotiate a settlement. But Toussaint was betrayed, captured, and imprisoned in France, where he died in 1803. Nevertheless, the rebels' new government prevailed. In 1804, the liberated country was renamed Haiti, and Toussaint became the symbol of its fight for liberty.

William Wilberforce (1759–1833)

The chief spokesman for the abolition of slavery in Parliament, William Wilberforce was the best-known advocate of the British abolition movement. Eloquent, wealthy, and a member of the House of Commons from 1780 to 1825, he occupied the ideal position to speak out for the cause. Although he initially faced enormous opposition, he guided the bill through Parliament that ended Britain's involvement in the slave trade in 1807.

Born to a wealthy family in Hull in 1759, he studied at Cambridge University and was elected to the House of Commons when he was only twenty-one. In his youth, he enjoyed a carefree social life, but in his mid-twenties, he began to take a profound interest in religion, which led him to associate with several evangelical leaders, including the former slave trader John Newton. As a result, he soon became a dedicated evangelical Christian, a generous philanthropist, and a devoted advocate of several humanitarian and reform causes, including the abolition of slavery.

Realizing that opposition from planters and other colonial interests was too strong for a direct attack on slavery to succeed, Wilberforce and the other abolitionists with whom he allied—including Thomas Clarkson and Granville Sharp—decided to try to end the slave trade first. Wilberforce introduced a bill to outlaw British participation in the slave trade in 1789, but despite his eloquence and influence, he could not get enough support to get it placed on the legislative agenda. Building support among his colleagues, he reintroduced the resolution each year until the House of Commons passed it in 1792. The House of Lords, however, vetoed it. Britain's almost continual war with France during the next fourteen years impeded the abolition cause. Because France would dominate the market after Britain's withdrawal from the slave trade, many regarded the demand for abolition as unpatriotic. Nevertheless, Wilberforce persisted, and in 1807 both houses of Parliament passed the bill to end British participation in the slave trade, effective on May 1, 1807.

Despite this victory, there was little public or political support for the abolition of slavery itself. After trying to strengthen enforcement of the ban on transporting slaves, Wilberforce began openly attacking slavery in 1815. While deteriorating health kept him from campaigning with the same vigor he had exerted for ending the trade, he and other abolitionists began to make inroads on public opinion. In 1823, he became the founding chair of the Anti-Slavery Committee, which led the anti-slavery campaign for the next decade. He resigned from the House of Commons in 1825, at age sixty-six, but he remained an ardent opponent of slavery until his death on July 29, 1833, three days after Parliament passed the law abolishing slavery throughout the British Empire.

Thomas Clarkson (1760–1846)

Thomas Clarkson played a crucial role in the British abolitionist movement. His research and fact-finding missions provided much of the ammunition that turned public opinion against the slave trade and convinced Parliament to abolish it in 1807.

Clarkson was born in 1760 in Wisbech, England, where his father was headmaster at a grammar school. Though he came from a relatively poor family, he won a scholarship to Cambridge University, where a writing assignment set the direction of his life. While seeking information for an essay on the subject, "Is it right to make slaves of others against their will?" Clarkson found there was little factual material about the slave trade or slavery. Among the little he discovered was Anthony Benezet's *Some Historical Account of Guinea* (see previous biography), which convinced him of the immorality of the slave trade and introduced him to the network of Quaker abolitionists. Clarkson's essay, written in Latin, won a prize, but it also motivated him to dedicate his life to collecting information about the traffic and educating others so it could be abolished.

In his quest for information, Clarkson visited many seaports, boarded ships, interviewed sailors and others connected with the slave traffic, and sometimes was handled roughly by those who did not like his inquiries. He was particularly interested in mortality among slaves and crew members. Clarkson used his findings to argue against the slave trade in essays that were published by the London Abolition Committee, of which he was a charter member. He also provided valuable information to William Wilberforce, leader of the abolitionist battle in Parliament (see previous biography), sometimes bringing informants from Liverpool to testify before parliamentary committees. Clarkson's best-known book, the two-volume *History of the Rise, Progress and Accomplishment of the Abolition of the African Slave Trade by the British Parliament,* published in 1808, marked the successful conclusion of the first phase of his work.

With the slave trade abolished, British abolitionists turned their attention to the abolition of slavery, organizing the Anti-Slavery Committee in 1823. When illness forced Wilberforce to step down as chair in 1830, Clarkson took over and directed the British abolitionist struggle until 1833, when Parliament abolished slavery throughout the British Empire. He died in 1846.

Joseph Wright (ca. 1810–1850s)

Joseph Wright was one of thousands of Africans enslaved during the civil wars of the Oyo Empire and rescued by the British anti-slave-trade squadron during the 1820s. He must have been about fifteen years old when the walled town of Oba (Owu), in what is now southwestern Nigeria, was captured by rival forces in 1825 or 1826. As the attackers overran the town, killing its leaders, elderly, and infants, many inhabitants tried to flee but were captured. Wright and his brothers were among the hundreds of captives tied together with ropes and marched away.

At markets along the way, Wright and his brothers were sold and separated from each other. He was sold a few times more before finally reaching Lagos in 1827, where he was sold to Portuguese traders and put aboard a ship destined for Brazil. Not long after its departure, however, the ship was captured by the British anti-slave-trade squadron. After about a month at sea, Wright arrived at Freetown, Sierra Leone, and was sent to the village of York. There he went to school, learned English, converted to Christianity, and in 1834 joined the Methodist Church. In 1839, he wrote a narrative about his enslavement and liberation, which was published in 1841 as part of a book titled *Ashantee and the Gold Coast* by John Beecham. The next year, the Methodist Missionary Society sent Wright to school in Britain, and upon his return in 1844 he became the Methodist Church's first native assistant missionary. He served as a missionary in Sierra Leone until his death in the late 1850s.

Samuel Ajayi Crowther (ca. 1806–91)

Ajayi was another African enslaved during Oyo's civil wars. Born in 1806 or 1807 in Osogon, part of the crumbling Yoruba state of Oyo, he was captured by slave raiders when he was thirteen. He was sold several times before he reached the coast at Lagos in December 1821, where he was resold and boarded on a Portuguese ship bound for Brazil. The ship was intercepted by the British anti-slave-trade novel squadron in April 1822, and the following month Ajayi and other liberated captives arrived at Sierra Leone (see document 3).

At Freetown in Sierra Leone, Ajayi learned English and practical skills such as carpentry. Converted to Christianity, he took the name Samuel Crowther at his baptism in 1825, to which he later added his

African name. After a few months' schooling in London in 1826, he became one of the first students to register at Freetown's Fourah Bay College, now the oldest institution of higher learning in West Africa. He married a fellow freed slave in 1829, was appointed a teacher by the government in 1830, and in 1834 returned to Fourah Bay College as a tutor.

At the request of missionaries, Crowther wrote the story of his capture and rescue, which was published in 1837. Sent to college by the Anglican Church Missionary Society (CMS) in 1842, he was ordained a priest the following year and subsequently served as a missionary to several areas in what is today Nigeria. After participating in two exploratory expeditions of the Niger River, he helped the CMS establish the Niger Mission in 1857 with an all-African staff. Meanwhile, he developed written forms for several West African languages and translated the Bible into Yoruba. He was consecrated bishop of the Niger Territory in 1864 and for the next fifteen years traveled widely establishing numerous churches, schools, and teacher-training colleges. During the 1880s, British imperialistic policy increasingly favored European officials over Africans, in religion as well as secular administration, and Crowther was replaced by a European prelate in 1890. Today recognized as an important founder of modern Nigeria, Crowther died on December 31, 1891.

Cinque (Singbe-Pih) (ca. 1817–79)

Introduced to late twentieth-century Americans through the movie *Amistad,* Cinque was an enslaved African who arrested national attention during 1839–41, as first a district court and then the U.S. Supreme Court considered his fate and that of fifty-two others delivered to Cuba in violation of international law.

The son of a Mende village leader in territory that is today part of Sierra Leone, Cinque was about twenty-one years old when fellow tribesmen seized and sold him to slave traders to satisfy a debt he owed them. Shipped to Havana in the Spanish colony of Cuba, he was purchased at auction by Pedro Montes and Jose Ruiz in the spring of 1839 and placed with their other purchases on a small schooner, *La Amistad* (meaning friendship), to return to their residence on the other side of the island. A storm blew the ship off course, and after a couple of weeks on what was to have been a two-day voyage, Cinque managed to free himself and the other slaves. They killed the captain and cook and easily subdued the owners while the two crew members fled in a lifeboat. Not knowing how to sail, Cinque had Montes and Ruiz pilot the ship in the direction of the rising sun, toward Africa. At night, however, the men furtively steered northwest, so that instead of moving steadily toward Africa, the ship zigzagged toward New York. On August 26, 1839, a U.S. Coast Guard vessel took the *Amistad* off the coast of Long Island and towed it to New London, Connecticut. The captives were lodged in the county jail at New Haven.

Although charged with murdering two men, the criminal case against Cinque and the other Africans was dismissed for jurisdictional reasons, and a civil case was set for January 1840 to determine if they should be returned to Montes and Ruiz. Lewis Tappan, a wealthy New York philanthropist and abolitionist, organized a committee to pay for and organize their defense. The committee hired a Connecticut attorney, Roger Baldwin, to represent them in court and help them file counter charges against Montes and Ruiz. Other abolitionists located an interpreter and taught the Africans English so they could tell their story in court.

In January 1840, government attorneys, supported by the Spanish embassy, argued before a U.S. district court that a 1795 treaty between the United States and Spain, in which each country agreed to return ships or goods of the other found on the high seas, required the United States to return the slaves to their owners. But citing an 1817 treaty between Spain and Great Britain banning the importation of slaves into Spanish colonies after 1820, the defense argued that the *Amistad* captives were not property, but free men. The court ruled in favor of the Africans and ordered them returned to their homeland.

Interceding on behalf of the Spaniards, however, President Martin Van Buren ordered the case to go to the Supreme Court. Former President John Quincy Adams joined Baldwin in arguing the case before the Supreme Court, which in March 1841 ordered the captives freed. Abolitionists lodged them in Farmington, Connecticut, until money could be raised for their return passage to Africa. Ten months later, in January 1842, the thirty-five surviving captives, accompanied by a band of missionaries, arrived at Freetown, Sierra Leone.

Cinque did not stay in the coastal missions, and all that is known about him after his repatriation is that he returned to a mission station thirty-seven years later, in 1879, to die.

Sarah Margru Kinson (ca. 1833–unknown)

One of four children who were part of the *Amistad's* captive cargo (see Cinque biography), Margru was born in Mandingo country in the Mende region of West Africa. She was only six years old when her father sold her to slave traders to pay a family debt. With other slaves from her region, she walked one hundred miles to the coast and was crammed into the notorious slave pens at Dunbomo to await the arrival of a slave ship that would take them across the Atlantic. Sold to European traders, she was shipped to Havana, Cuba, aboard a Portuguese slaver. Margru and two other girls were purchased by Pedro Montes and Jose Ruiz and taken onto the *Amistad* for another voyage.

After the slaves took control of the *Amistad* and the U.S. Coast Guard subsequently captured it, the girls were lodged with the other captives at the county jail in New Haven, Connecticut, to await the trials that would determine their fate. As news of the revolt and imprisonment flashed across the country, thousands of curious people thronged to the jail to get a look at the Africans. Concerned about the effect the uproar might have on the children, Lewis Tappan, the abolitionist who organized aid for the captives' legal defense, arranged for the girls to stay in the home of the jailer and his wife, where they served as domestic servants.

After the Supreme Court set them free, Margru and her fellow Africans were housed, fed, and tutored by abolitionists while money was raised for their passage back home. It was then that Margru was given the name Sarah Kinson. Finally, in November 1841, more than two and a half years after their first crossing of the Atlantic, she and the other thirty-five surviving *Amistad* captives were returned to Africa, arriving at Freetown, Sierra Leone, in January 1842.

Sarah and the other two girls lived with a missionary couple who had accompanied them, John and Eliza Raymond, at the new mission station they established, Kaw Mendi. She became a Christian and exhibited such promise that Raymond wanted her to be educated in America so she could head the female department of their school. In 1846, with the help of Lewis Tappan, a primary benefactor of Oberlin College, Sarah began her formal education in the community school at Oberlin, Ohio, and was later admitted to the Ladies' Department of the college. Returning to Kaw Mendi in November 1849, she became "schoolmistress" of the mission's new girls' school.

Biographical Sketches

In 1852, Sarah married Edward Green, an African who had been educated at British mission schools in Freetown. They left Kaw Mendi in January 1855 to establish their own mission, but after a few months her husband was dismissed as a missionary for inappropriate behavior. The record of Sarah's life ends at this point, but she evidently had a son by a second marriage, who was educated in America but died before he could return to Africa. Sarah Kinson evidently continued teaching, for a grammar school is named after her in Bonthe, Sierra Leone.

PRIMARY DOCUMENTS OF THE ATLANTIC SLAVE TRADE

Document 1
Capture and Enslavement of Equiano, 1750s

Olaudah Equiano was one of only a few enslaved Africans who were able to write of their experiences (see biographical sketch). Enslaved in what is today southeastern Nigeria during the 1750s when he was eleven years old, he wrote his account some thirty-five years later. Although his memory may have been colored by later experiences and become more sentimental, his story, first published in 1789 as *The Interesting Narrative of the Life of Olaudah Equiano*, is nevertheless stirring and heartrending. Reprinted by permission from Harcourt Publishers. From Paul Edwards, ed., *Equiano's Travels* (Oxford: Harcourt, 1996), 13–21.

My father, besides many slaves, had a numerous family of which seven lived to grow up, including myself and a sister who was the only daughter. As I was the youngest of the sons I became, of course, the greatest favorite with my mother and was always with her; and she used to take particular pains to form my mind. I was trained up from my earliest years in the art of war, my daily exercise was shooting and throwing javelins, and my mother adorned me with emblems after the manner of our greatest warriors. In this way I grew up till I was turned the age of 11 . . .

One day, when all our people were gone out to their works as usual and only I and my dear sister were left to mind the house, two

Note: In these selections, excerpted from primary documents and published sources, British spellings have been changed to American, some antiquated terminology has been altered, and punctuation has been adjusted to make the text more readable.

men and a woman got over our walls and in a moment seized us both, and without giving us time to cry out or make resistance they stopped our mouths and ran off with us into the nearest wood. Here they tied our hands and continued to carry us as far as they could till night came on, when we reached a small house where the robbers halted for refreshment and spent the night. We were then unbound but were unable to take any food, and being quite overpowered by fatigue and grief, our only relief was some sleep . . .

The next morning we left the house and continued traveling all the day. For a long time we had kept to the woods, but at last we came into a road which I believed I knew. I had now some hopes of being delivered, for we had advanced but a little way before I discovered some people at a distance, on which I began to cry out for their assistance. But my cries had no other effect than to make them tie me faster and stop my mouth, and then they put me into a large sack. They also stopped my sister's mouth and tied her hands, and in this manner we proceeded till we were out of the sight of these people. When we went to rest the following night they offered us some victuals, but we refused it, and the only comfort we had was in being in one another's arms all that night and bathing each other with our tears. . . .

The next day . . . my sister and I were then separated while we lay clasped in each other's arms. It was in vain that we besought them not to part us; she was torn from me and immediately carried away . . . I cried and grieved continually, and for several days I did not eat anything but what they forced into my mouth.

At length, after many days' traveling, during which I had often changed masters, I got into the hands of a chieftain in a very pleasant country. This man had two wives and some children, and they all used me extremely well and did all they could to comfort me, particularly the first wife, who was something like my mother. Although I was a great many days' journey from my father's house, yet these people spoke exactly the same language with us. This first master . . . was a smith, and my principal employment was working his bellows . . .

I was there I suppose about a month, and they at last used to trust me some little distance from the house. This liberty I used in embracing every opportunity to inquire the way to my own home; and I also sometimes, for the same purpose, went with the maidens in the cool of the evenings to bring pitchers of water from the springs for the use of the house. I had also remarked where the sun rose in the morning and set in the evening as I had traveled along, and I had observed that my father's house was towards the rising of the sun. I therefore determined to seize the first opportunity of making my escape and to shape my course for that quarter . . .

While I was projecting my escape, one day an unlucky event happened which quite disconcerted my plan and put an end to my hopes. I used to be sometimes employed in assisting an elderly woman slave to cook and take care of the poultry, and one morning, while I was feeding some chickens, I happened to toss a small pebble at one of them, which hit it on the middle and directly killed it. . . . I expected an instant flogging, which to me was uncommonly dreadful, for I had seldom been beaten at home.

I therefore resolved to [flee], and accordingly I ran into a thicket that was [near]by and hid myself in the bushes. Soon afterwards my mistress and the slave returned, and not seeing me they searched all the house, but not finding me, and I not making answer when they called to me, they thought I had run away and the whole neighborhood was raised in the pursuit of me. In that part of the country (as in ours) the houses and villages were skirted with woods or shrubberies, and the bushes were so thick that a man could readily conceal himself in them so as to elude the strictest search. The neighbors continued the whole day looking for me . . . but they never discovered me, though they were often so near that I even heard their conjectures as they were looking about for me; and I now learned from them that any attempts to return home would be hopeless. Most of them supposed I had fled towards home, but the distance was so great and the way so intricate that they thought I could never reach it . . .

I heard frequent rustling among the leaves, and being pretty sure they were snakes I expected every instant to be stung by them. This increased my anguish and the horror of my situation became now quite insupportable. I at length quitted the thicket, very faint and hungry for I had not eaten or drank anything all the day, and crept to my master's kitchen from whence I set out at first . . . and laid myself down in the ashes with an anxious wish for death to relieve me from all my pains. I was scarcely awake in the morning when the old woman slave, who was the first up, came to light the fire and saw me in the fireplace. She was very much surprised to see me and could scarcely believe her own eyes. She now promised to intercede for me and went for her master, who soon after came, and, having slightly reprimanded me, ordered me to be taken care of and not ill-treated.

Soon after this my master's only daughter and child by his first wife sickened and died, which affected him so much that for some time he was almost frantic, and really would have killed himself had he not been watched and prevented. However, in a small time afterwards he recovered and I was again sold. I was now carried to the left of the sun's rising, through many different countries and a number of large woods. The people I was sold to used to carry me very often when I was tired either on their shoulders or on their backs. . . .

From the time I left my own nation I always found somebody that understood me till I came to the sea coast. The languages of different nations did not totally differ, nor were they so copious as those of the Europeans . . . They were therefore easily learned, and while I was journeying thus through Africa I acquired two or three different tongues. In this manner I had been traveling for a considerable time, when one evening, to my great surprise, whom should I see brought to the house where I was but my dear sister! As soon as she saw me she gave a loud shriek and ran into my arms . . . I was quite overpowered: neither of us could speak, but for a considerable time clung to each other in mutual embraces, unable to do anything but weep. . . . When these people knew we were brother and sister they indulged us to be together, and the man to whom I supposed we belonged lay with us, he in the middle while she and I held one another by the hands across his breast all night; and thus for a while we forgot our misfortunes in the joy of being together. But even this small comfort was soon to have an end, for scarcely had the fatal morning appeared when she was again torn from me forever! . . .

I did not long remain after my sister. I was again sold and carried through a number of places till, after traveling a considerable time, I came to a town called Tinmah in the most beautiful country I had yet seen in Africa. . . . Here I first saw and tasted coconuts, which I thought superior to any nuts I had ever tasted . . . Here I also saw and tasted for the first time sugar-cane. Their money consisted of little white shells the size of the finger-nail. I was sold here for 172 of them by a merchant who lived and brought me there. I had been about two or three days at his house when a wealthy widow, a neighbor of his, came there one evening and brought with her an only son, a young gentleman about my own age and size. Here they saw me; and, having taken a fancy to me, I was bought . . . and went home with them. . . .

The next day I was washed and perfumed, and when meal-time came I was led into the presence of my mistress, and ate and drank before her with her son. This filled me with astonishment; and I could scarce help expressing my surprise that the young gentleman should suffer me, who was bound, to eat with him who was free; and not only so, but that he would not at any time either eat or drink till I had taken first, because I was the eldest, which was agreeable to our custom. Indeed everything here, and all their treatment of me, made me forget that I was a slave. The language of these people resembled ours so nearly that we understood each other perfectly. They had also the very same customs as we. There were likewise slaves daily to attend us, while my young master and I with other boys sported with our darts and bows and arrows, as I had been used to do at home. In this resemblance to my former happy state I passed about two months, and I now began to think I was to be adopted into the family, and was beginning to be reconciled to my situation and to forget by degrees my misfortunes . . . [But] without the least previous knowledge, one morning early while my dear master and companion was still asleep, I was wakened out of my reverie . . . and hurried away . . .

All the nations and people I had hitherto passed through resembled our own in their manner, customs, and language, but I came at length to a country the inhabitants of which differed from us in all those particulars. I was very much struck with this difference, especially when I came among a people who did not circumcise and ate without washing their hands. They cooked also in iron pots and had European cutlasses and crossbows, which were unknown to us, and fought with their fists amongst themselves. Their women were not so modest as ours, for they ate and drank and slept with their men. But above all, I was amazed to see no sacrifices or offerings among them. In some of those places the people ornamented themselves with scars, and likewise filed their teeth very sharp. They wanted sometimes to ornament me in the same manner, but I would not suffer them, hoping that I might some time be among a people who did not thus disfigure themselves, as I thought they did.

At last I came to the banks of a large river, which was covered with canoes in which the people appeared to live with their household utensils and provisions of all kinds. I was beyond measure astonished at this, as I had never before seen any water larger than a pond or a rivulet, and my surprise was mingled with no small fear when I was put into one of these canoes and we began to paddle and move along the river. We continued going on thus till night, and when we came to land and made fires on the banks, each family by themselves, some dragged their canoes on shore, others stayed and cooked in theirs and laid in them all night. . . . [A]fter the morning meal we embarked again and proceeded as before. . . . Thus I continued to travel, sometimes by land, sometimes by water, through different countries and various nations, till at the end of six or seven months after I had been kidnapped I arrived at the sea coast.

Document 2
Mungo Park Accompanying a Slave Coffle in West Africa, 1797

One of the earliest European explorers in the interior of West Africa was the Scottish medical doctor and explorer Mungo Park, who was commissioned by the British African Association to explore the Niger River in 1795–97. Like many explorers after him, Park was an abolitionist seeking opportunities for legitimate commerce to replace the slave trade. Traveling up the Gambia River, he learned a few African languages, was taken prisoner, and eventually joined a slave caravan to make his way back to the coast. His is one of the few accounts that describe a slave march from the interior to the coast. Reprinted by permission of the Carnegie Institution. From Elisabeth Donnan, *Documents Illustrative of the Slave Trade to America,* vol. 2 (Washington, D.C.: Carnegie Institution, 1930–35), 632–42.

On my arrival at Kamalia, I was conducted to the house of . . . Karfa Taura . . . He was collecting a coffle [caravan] of slaves with the view to sell them to the Europeans on the Gambia, as soon as the rains should be over. . . .

As I was one day conversing with the slaves . . . one of them begged me to give him some victuals. I told him I was a stranger and had none to give. He replied, "I gave you victuals when you was hungry. Have you forgot the man who brought you milk at Karrankalla? But," added he with a sigh, "the irons were not then upon my legs!" I immediately recollected him and begged some groundnuts from Karfa to give him . . . [in] return for his former kindness. He told me that he had been taken away by the Bambara the day after the battle of Joka, and sent to Segu, where he had been purchased by his present master. . . . Three more of these slaves were from Kaarta, and one from Wassela, all of them prisoners of war. . . .

In the beginning of December [1796], Karfa proposed to complete his purchase of slaves, and for this purpose collected all the debts . . . On the 19th . . . he departed for Kancaba, a large town on the banks of the Niger, and a great slave market. Most of the slaves who are sold at Kancaba come from Bambara. . . . To avoid the expense and danger of keeping all . . . prisoners at Segu, [merchants] commonly send them in small parties to be sold at the different trading towns.

All these unfortunate beings are considered as strangers and foreigners, who have no right to the protection of the law and may be treated with severity or sold to a stranger, according to the pleasure of their owners. There are, indeed, regular markets where slaves of this description are bought and sold, and the value of a slave . . . increases in proportion to his distance from his native kingdom. For when slaves are only a few days' journey from the place of their nativity, they frequently effect their escape, but when one or more kingdoms intervene . . . they are more readily reconciled to their situation. On this account, the unhappy slave is frequently transferred from one dealer to another until he has lost all hopes of returning to his native kingdom. The slaves which are purchased by the Europeans on the coasts are chiefly of this description; a few of them are collected in the petty wars . . . which take place near the coast. But by far the greater number are brought down in large caravans from the inland countries . . .

On the 24th of January [1797], Karfa returned to Kamalia with a number of people, and thirteen prime slaves which he had purchased. . . . , prisoners of war . . . taken by the Bambara army in the kingdoms of Wassela and Kaarta, and carried to Segu, where some of them had remained three years in irons. From Segu they were sent . . . up the Niger in two large canoes and offered for sale . . . [T]he greater number of the captives were bartered for gold dust, and the remainder sent forward to Kankaree.

Eleven of them confessed to me that they had been slaves from their infancy; but the other two refused to give any account of their former condition. They were all very inquisitive, but they viewed me at first with looks of horror and repeatedly asked if my countrymen were cannibals. They were very desirous to know what became of the slaves after they had crossed the salt water. I told them that they were employed in cultivating the land, but they would not believe me. One of them, putting his hand upon the ground, said with great simplicity, "Have you really got such ground as this to set your feet upon?" A deeply rooted idea, that the whites purchase Negroes for the purpose of devouring them . . . naturally makes the slaves contemplate a journey towards the coast with great terror. . . . [To prevent escape] they are commonly secured by putting the right leg of one and the left of another into the same pair of fetters. By supporting the fetters with a string they can walk, though very slowly. Every four slaves are likewise fastened together by the necks with a strong rope of twisted thongs, and in the night an additional pair of fetters is put on their hands and some-times a light iron chain passed round their necks.

Such of them as evince marks of discontent are secured in a differ-ent manner. A thick billet of wood is cut, about three feet long, and a smooth notch being made upon one side of it. The ankle of the slave is bolted to the smooth part by means of a strong iron staple, one prong of which passes on each side of the ankle. All these fetters and bolts are made from native iron. In the present case they were put on by the blacksmith as soon as the slaves arrived from Kancaba, and were not taken off until the morning on which the coffle departed for Gambia.

In other respects, the treatment of the slaves during their stay at Kamalia was far from being harsh or cruel. They were led out in their fetters every morning to the shade of the tamarind tree, where they were encouraged to play at games of hazard and sing diverting songs to keep up their spirits. For though some of them sustained the hardships of their situation with amazing fortitude, the greater part were very much dejected and would sit all day in a sort of sullen melancholy, with their eyes fixed upon the ground. In the evening their irons were exam-ined and their hand fetters put on, after which they were conducted into two large huts, where they were guarded during the night by Karfa's domestic slaves. . . .

April 19th. The long wished-for day of our departure was at length arrived, and the . . . [merchants] having taken the irons from their slaves, assembled with them at the door of Karfa's house, where the bundles were all tied up and every one had his load assigned him. The coffle on its departure from Kamalia consisted of twenty-seven slaves . . . We were afterwards joined by five at Maraboo and three at Bala, making in all thirty-five slaves. The free men were fourteen in number, but most of them had one or two wives and some domestic slaves, and the schoolmaster, who was now upon his return for Worakoo. [He] . . . took with him eight of his scholars so that the number of free people and domestic slaves amounted to thirty-eight, and the whole amount of the coffle was seventy-three. . . .

As many of the slaves had remained for years in irons, the sudden exertion of walking quick, with heavy loads upon their heads, occasioned spasmodic contractions of their legs, and we had not proceeded above a mile before it was found necessary to take two of them from the rope and allow them to walk more slowly until we reached Maraboo, a walled village where some people were waiting to join the coffle. Here we stopped about two hours to allow the strangers time to pack up their provisions and then continued our route to Bala.

As this was the first town beyond the limits of [the] Mandinka, greater etiquette than usual was observed. Every person was ordered to keep in his proper station, and we marched towards the town in a sort of procession. . . . In front [were] five or six singing men; these were followed by the other free people; then came the slaves fastened in the usual way by a rope round their necks, four of them to a rope and a man with a spear between each four. After them came the domestic slaves, and in the rear the women of free condition, wives of the [merchants] . . . As soon as we had crossed the river . . . The guides and young men were accordingly placed in the van, the women and slaves in the center, and the free men in the rear. . . .

In the afternoon [Apr. 28] we passed several villages, at none of which could we procure a lodging. And in the twilight we received information that two hundred Jallonkas had assembled . . . with a view to plunder the coffle. This induced us to alter our course, and we traveled with great secrecy until midnight, when we approached a town called Koba. Before we entered the town, the names of all the people belonging to the coffle were called over, and a free man and three slaves were found to be missing. Every person immediately concluded that the slaves had murdered the free man and made their escape. It was therefore agreed that six people should go back as far as the last village and endeavor to find his body or collect some information concerning the slaves. In the mean time the coffle was ordered to lie concealed in a cotton field. . . .

It was towards morning before the six men returned having heard nothing of the man or the slaves. As none of us had tasted victuals for the last twenty-four hours, it was agreed that we should go into Koba and endeavor to procure some provisions. We accordingly entered the town before it was quite day, and Karfa purchased from the chief man, for three strings of beads, a considerable quantity of ground nuts, which we roasted and ate for breakfast. We were afterwards provided with huts, and rested here for the day. . . .

The information that we received concerning the Jallonkas, who intended to rob the coffle, was this day confirmed, and we were forced to remain here until the afternoon of the 30th when Karfa hired a number of people to protect us, . . . Departing . . . on the day following, we crossed a high ridge of mountains to the west of the Black river and traveled over a rough stony country until sunset, when we arrived at . . . a small village in the district of Woradoo. Here we shook out the last handful of meal from our dry provision bags, this being the second day since we crossed the Black river that we had traveled from morning until night without tasting one morsel of food . . .

May 13th. In the morning, . . . a coffle of slaves belonging to some Serawoolli traders crossed the river and agreed to proceed with us to . . . the capital of Dentila. . . . We . . . traveled with great expedition through the woods until noon, when one of the Serawoolli slaves dropped a load from his head, for which he was smartly whipped. The load was replaced, but he had not proceeded above a mile before he let it fall a second time, for which he received the same punishment. After this he traveled in great pain until about two o'clock, when we stopped to breathe a little by a pool of water, the day being remarkably hot. The poor slave was now so completely exhausted that his master was obliged to release him from the rope, for he lay motionless on the ground. A Serawoolli therefore undertook to remain with him and endeavor to bring him to the town during the cool of the night. In the meanwhile, we continued our route and after a very hard day's travel arrived at Baniserile late in the evening . . .

About eight o'clock the same evening, the Serawoolli who had been left in the woods to take care of the fatigued slave returned and told us that he was dead. The general opinion, however, was that he himself had killed him or left him to perish on the road, for the Serawoollis are said to be infinitely more cruel in their treatment of slaves than the Mandinka . . .

On the morning of the 20th we entered the Tenda Wilderness. The woods were very thick . . . About ten o'clock we met a coffle of twenty-six people and seven loaded donkeys returning from [the] Gambia. Most of the men were armed with muskets and had broad belts of scarlet cloth over their shoulders and European hats upon their heads. They informed us that there was very little demand for slaves on the coast, as no vessel had arrived for some months past. On hearing this, the Serawoolis who had traveled with us . . . separated themselves and their slaves from the coffle. They had not, they said, the means of maintaining their slaves in Gambia until a vessel should arrive . . . We continued our route through the wilderness and traveled all day through a rugged country, covered with extensive thickets of bamboo . . .

Here . . . one of the slaves belonging to the coffle, who had traveled with great difficulty for the last three days, was found unable to proceed any farther. His master, a singing man, proposed therefore to exchange him for a young slave girl belonging to one of the townspeople. The poor girl was ignorant of her fate until . . . coming with some other young women to see the coffle set out, her master took her by the hand and delivered her to the singing man. Never was a face of serenity more suddenly changed into one of the deepest distress. The terror she manifested on having the load put upon her head and the rope fastened round her neck, and the sorrow with which she bade adieu to her companions, were truly affecting . . .

Being now [June 2, 1797] within a short distance of Pisania, from whence my journey originally commenced, and learning that my friend Karfa was not likely to meet with an immediate opportunity of selling his slaves on the Gambia, it occurred to me to suggest to him that he would find it for his interest to leave them at Jindey until a market should offer. Karfa agreed with me in this opinion and hired from the chief man of the town huts for their accommodation and a piece of land on which to employ them in raising corn and other provisions for their maintenance. With regard to himself, he declared that he would not quit me until my departure from Africa. We set out accordingly—Karfa, myself, and one of the Fulbe belonging to the coffle—early on the morning of the 9th. But although I was now approaching the end of my tedious and toilsome journey and expected in another day to meet with countrymen and friends, I could not part for the last time with my unfortunate fellow-travelers, doomed to . . . a life of captivity and slav-

ery in a foreign land, without great emotion. . . . We parted with recip-
rocal expressions of regret and benediction. My good wishes and
prayers were all I could bestow upon them, and it afforded me some
consolation to be told that they [understood] I had no more to give . . .

On the 15th [June], the ship of Charlestown, an American vessel
commanded by Mr. Charles Harris, entered the river. She came for
slaves, intending to touch at Goree to fill up and to proceed from thence
to South Carolina. . . . I therefore immediately engaged my passage in
this vessel for America, and having taken leave of Dr. Laidley, to whose
kindness I was so largely indebted, and my other friends on the river, I
embarked at Kaye on the 17th day of June.

Our passage down the river was tedious and fatiguing, and the
weather was so hot, moist, and unhealthy, that before our arrival at
Goree, four of the seamen, the surgeon, and three of the slaves, had
died of fevers. At Goree we were detained, for want of provisions, until
the beginning of October.

The number of slaves received on board this vessel, both on the
Gambia and at Goree, was one hundred and thirty, of whom about
twenty-five had been . . . free . . . in Africa, as most of those . . . could
write a little Arabic. Nine of them had become captives in the religious
war between Abdulkader and Damel. . . . Two of the others had seen me
as I passed through Bondou, and many of them had heard of me in the
interior countries. My conversation with them in their native language
gave them great comfort, and as the surgeon was dead, I consented to
act in a medical capacity in his room for the remainder of the voyage.
They had in truth need of every consolation in my power to bestow. Not
that I observed any wanton acts of cruelty practiced either by the master or the seamen towards them, but the mode of confining and securing Negroes in the American slave ships, owing chiefly to [small] crews,
made these poor creatures to suffer greatly, and a general sickness prevailed amongst them. Besides the three who died on the Gambia and six
or eight while we remained at Goree, eleven perished at sea, and many
of the survivors were reduced to a very weak and emaciated condition.

In the midst of these distresses, the vessel, after having been three
weeks at sea, became so extremely leaky as to require constant exertion
at the pumps. It was found necessary, therefore, to take some of the
ablest of the Negro men out of irons and employ them at this labor, in
which they were often worked beyond their strength. . . . We directed

our course for Antigua and fortunately made that island in about thirty-five days after our departure from Goree. Yet even at this juncture we narrowly escaped destruction, for on approaching the northwest side of the island, we struck on Diamond Rock and got into St. John's harbor with great difficulty. The vessel was afterwards condemned as unfit for sea, and the slaves, as I have heard, were ordered to be sold for the benefit of the owners.

Document 3
Enslavement and Liberation of Samuel Ajayi Crowther, 1820–22

Kidnapped from the interior of Nigeria in March 1820, thirteen-year-old Ajayi was sold to a series of masters over the next year and a half as he was steadily moved toward the coast and European slavers. Within days of being placed aboard a Portuguese ship bound for Brazil, however, he was rescued by the British anti-slave-trade squadron. Taken with other freed slaves to Freetown, Sierra Leone, he converted to Christianity, took the name Samuel Crowther, and became a missionary to his Nigerian homeland (see biographical sketch). His recollections, from which the following selection is taken, were written in 1837. Reprinted by permission of Waveland Press, Inc. From Philip D. Curtin, ed., *Africa Remembered: Narratives by West Africans from the Era of the Slave Trade*, 2d ed. (Prospect Heights, Ill.: Waveland Press, Inc., 1967; reissued 1997), 298–316. All rights reserved.

For some years, war had been carried on in my Oyo Country, which was always attended with much devastation and bloodshed; the women, such men as had surrendered or were caught, with the children were taken captives. The enemies who carried on these wars were principally the Oyo Mohamedans, with whom my country abounds, the Fulbe, and such foreign slaves as had escaped from their owners, joined together making a formidable force of about 20,000 . . . They had no other employment but selling slaves to the Spaniards and Portuguese on the coast.

The morning in which my town, Osogun, [was taken], . . . we were preparing breakfast without any apprehension when . . . a rumor was spread in the town that the enemies had approached . . . It was not long after when they had almost surrounded the town to prevent any escape of the inhabitants. The town [was] rudely fortified with a wooden fence about four miles in circumference, containing about

12,000 inhabitants, which would produce 3,000 fighting men. The inhabitants not being duly prepared . . . the enemies entered the town after about three or four hours' resistance. . . . [W]omen, some with three, four, or six children clinging to their arms, with the infants on their backs and such baggage as they could carry on their heads, [ran] as fast as they could through prickly shrubs . . . [but] were overtaken and caught . . . with a noose of rope thrown over the neck of every individual, to be led in the manner of goats tied together, under the drove of one man. In many cases a family was violently divided between three or four enemies, who each led his away to see one another no more. Your humble servant was thus caught—with his mother, two sisters (one an infant about ten months old), and a cousin—while endeavoring to escape in the manner above described. . . . The last view I had of my father was when he came from the fight to give us the signal to flee . . . I learned some time afterward that he was killed in another battle.

Our conquerors were Oyo Mohamedans, who led us through the town [and] hostilely separated my cousin from our number. . . . The town [was set] on fire . . . The flame was very high. We were led by my grandfather's house, already desolate . . . [and then led out of town and marched to] Iseyin, the rendezvous of the enemies, about twenty miles from our town. . . . The aged women were to be greatly pitied, not being able to walk so fast as their children and grandchildren; they were often threatened with being put to death upon the spot. . . .

[T]he next morning . . . we were brought to the Chief of our captors . . . as trophies at his feet. . . . [A] separation took place, when my sister and I fell to the share of the Chief and my mother and the infant to the victors. . . . [I was] bartered for a horse in Iseyin that very day [and] . . . separated from my mother and sister . . . [After] two months, . . . the horse, which was then only taken on trial, not being approved of, I was restored to the Chief, who took me to Dada, where I had the happiness to meet my mother and infant sister again . . . Here I lived for about three months, going for grass for horses with my fellow captives. . . .

[One] unhappy evening . . . I was added to the number of many other captives, enfettered, to be led to the market-town early the next morning. . . . [T]he traders . . . loaded the men slaves with baggage. With one hand chained to the neck, we left the town. . . . After a few days' travel, we came to the market-town Ijaye. Here I saw many who had escaped in our town to this place, or those who were in search of their relations to set at liberty as many as they had the means of redeeming. . . . I was sold to a Mohamedan woman, with whom I traveled to many towns in our way to the Popo country, on the coast, much resorted to by the Portuguese, to buy slaves. . . . Now and then my mistress would speak with me and her son, that we should by and by go to the Popo country, where we should buy tobacco, and other fine things, to sell at our return. Now, thought I, this was the signal of my being sold to the Portuguese . . . I determined . . . I would not go to the Popo country; but would make an end of myself one way or another. . . . I attempted strangling myself with my band but had not courage enough to close the noose tight . . . I determined, next, that I would leap out of the canoe into the river . . . Thus was I thinking, when my owner . . . sold me . . . After my price had been counted before my own eyes, I was delivered up to my new owners . . . [and] we set out for Ijebu, the third dialect from mine.

[A]t Ikereku-iwere . . . I was bartered for tobacco, rum, and other articles. I remained here in fetters, alone, for some time before my owner could get as many slaves as he wanted. . . . I had to remain alone again in another town . . . for about two months. From hence I was brought, after a few days' walk, to a slave-market called Ikosi, on the coast, on the bank of a river . . . The sight of the river terrified me exceedingly, for I had never seen anything like it in my life. . . . [B]artered again for tobacco, I became another owner's. Nothing now terrified me more than the river, and the thought of going into another world. . . . Night coming on and the men having very little time to spare, [they] soon carried me into the canoe and placed me among the corn-bags and supplied me with [food]. Almost the same position I was placed I remained, . . . quite confused in my thoughts, waiting only every moment our arrival at the new world, which we did not reach till about 4 o'clock in the morning. . . . [D]uring the whole night's voyage in the canoe, not a single thought of leaping into the river had entered my mind; but on the contrary, the fear of the river occupied my thoughts.

[At] Lagos, I was permitted to go any way I pleased, there being no way of escape on account of the river. . . . One part of the town was occupied by the Portuguese and Spaniards who had come to buy slaves. [But for] more than three months, I never once saw a White Man . . . [H]aving no more hope of ever going to my country again, I patiently took whatever came, although it was not without great fear and trembling that I received, for the first time, the touch of a White Man, who examined me whether I was sound or not. Men and boys were at first chained together, with a chain of about six fathoms in length, thrust through an iron fetter on the neck of every individual and fastened at both ends with padlocks. In this situation the boys suffered the most. The men sometimes, getting angry, would draw the chain so violently as [to cause] bruises on [the boys'] poor little necks; especially [at night], when they drew the chain so close to ease themselves of its weight in order to be able to lie more conveniently, that we were almost suffocated or bruised to death in a room with one door, which was fastened as soon as we entered in, with no other passage for [ventilation] than the openings under the eavesdrop. Very often at night, when two or three individuals quarreled or fought, the whole drove suffered punishment without any distinction. At last, we boys had the happiness to be separated from the men . . .

About this time, [we learned that] the English were cruising the coast . . . [W]e were embarked at night in canoes from Lagos to the beach, and on the following morning were put on board the vessel, which immediately sailed away. The crew being busy embarking us, 187 in number, had no time to give us either breakfast or supper . . . On the next morning [we] found ourselves in the hands of new conquerors, whom we at first very much dreaded, they being armed with long swords. . . . [C]alled up from the hold, we were astonished to find ourselves among two very large men-of-war and several other brigs . . . who captured us on the 7th of April, 1822, on the river Lagos.

Our owner was bound with his sailors . . . We in a short time took the liberty of ranging about the vessel in search of plunder of every kind. Now we began to entertain a good opinion of our conquerors. Very soon after breakfast, we were divided into several of the vessels around us. This was cause of new fears, not knowing where our misery would end. Being now, as it were, one family, we began to take leave of those who were first transshipped, not knowing what would become of them and ourselves. About this time six of us . . . kept very close together, that we might be carried away at the same time. It was not long before we six were conveyed into the *Myrmidon* [a ship belonging to the anti-slave-trade squadron], in which we discovered not any trace of those who were transshipped before us. . . .

In a few days we were quite at home on the man-of-war. Being only six in number, we were . . . soon furnished with clothes. Our Portuguese owner and his son were brought over into the same vessel, bound in fetters, and thinking that I should no more get into his hand, I had the boldness to strike him on the head . . . His vessel was towed along by the man-of-war with the remainder of the slaves therein. But after a few weeks, the slaves were transshipped from her and, being stripped of her rigging, the schooner was left alone on the ocean . . .

One of the brigs which contained a part of the slaves was wrecked on a sand-bank, [but] happily, another vessel was near, and all the lives were saved. It was not long before another brig sunk during a tempest, with all the slaves and sailors with the exception of about five of the latter, who were found in a boat after four or five days . . . and were so feeble that they could not stand on their feet. One hundred and two of our number were lost on this occasion.

After nearly two months and a half cruising the coast, we were landed at Sierra Leone on the 17th day of June, 1822. The same day we were sent to Bathurst . . . Here we had the pleasure of meeting many of our country people . . . [who] assured us of our liberty and freedom.

Document 4
Ayuba's Capture and Return to Africa, 1730–35

The story of Ayuba Suleiman Diallo (aka Job, in English circles) is most unusual. An educated Muslim from an influential family in the interior of West Africa, he was captured and enslaved while returning home after himself selling slaves on the coast. Ending up a slave in Maryland, his intelligence, education, and abilities were recognized by an Englishman who secured his freedom and arranged his return to Africa (see biographical sketch). Because Ayuba was unable to write well in English, his story was told by his rescuer, Thomas Bluett, who published the account in 1734 under the title *Some Memoirs of the Life of Job, the Son of Solomon the High Priest of Boonda in Africa.* Reprinted by permission of Waveland Press, Inc. From Philip D. Curtin, ed., *Africa Remembered: Narratives by West Africans from the Era of the Slave Trade,* 2d ed. (Prospect Heights, Ill.: Waveland Press, Inc., 1967; reissued 1997), 34–59. All rights reserved.

In February 1730, Job's father hearing of an English ship at Gambia River, sent him with two servants to attend him to sell two Negroes and to buy paper and some other necessaries, but desired him not to venture over the river because the . . . Mandinka are enemies to the people of Futa. . . . Job . . . sent back . . . two servants to let [his father] know that he intended to go farther. Accordingly, having agreed with another man . . . who understood the Mandinka language to go with him as his interpreter, he crossed the River Gambia and disposed of his Negroes for some cows. As he was returning home, he stopped for some refreshment at the house of an old acquaintance . . . The weather being hot, he hung up his arms in the house, while he refreshed himself. . . .

It happened that a company of the Mandinka . . . passing by at that time and observing him unarmed, rushed in . . . [through] a back door and pinned Job [down] . . . together with his interpreter, who is a slave in Maryland still [Lamine, the interpreter, was ransomed in 1738 and returned to Africa]. They then shaved their heads and beards, which Job and his man resented as the highest indignity, though the Mandinka meant no more by it than to make them appear like slaves taken in war. On the 27th of February, 1730, they carried them to Captain Pike at Gambia, who purchased them, and on the first of March they were put on board. Soon after Job found means to acquaint Captain Pike that he was the same person that came to trade with him a few days before, and after what manner he had been taken. Upon this, Captain Pike gave him leave to redeem himself and his man, and Job sent . . . [word] to [his] father . . . that he might take some course to have him set at liberty. But it being a fortnight's journey . . . and the ship sailing in about a week, Job was brought with the rest of the slaves to Annapolis in Maryland. . . . Job [was sold] to one Mr. Tolsey in Kent Island in Maryland, who put him to work in making tobacco, but he was soon convinced that Job had never been used to such labor. He . . . showed more and more uneasiness under this exercise and at last grew sick, being no way able to bear it so that his master was obliged to find easier work for him and therefore put him to tend the cattle. Job would often leave the cattle and withdraw into the woods to pray; but a white boy frequently watched him, and whilst he was at his devotion would mock him, and throw dirt in his face. . . .

[Job] resolved to travel at a venture, thinking he might possibly be taken up by some master who would use him better or otherwise meet with some lucky accident to divert or abate his grief. Accordingly, he traveled through the woods till he came to the County of Kent, . . . [where he] was put in prison . . .

This happened about the beginning of June . . . when I [Thomas Bluett] . . . was attending the courts there and heard of Job, . . . and desired to see him. He was brought into the tavern to us but could not speak one word of English. Upon our talking and making signs to him, he wrote a line or two before us, and when he read it [he] pronounced the words Allah and Mohammed, . . . and his refusing a glass of wine we offered him, we perceived he was a Muslim, but could not imagine of what country he was or how he got thither, for by his affable carriage and the easy composure of his countenance we could perceive he was no common slave.

When Job had been some time confined, an old Negro man who . . . could speak the Jalloff language, which Job also understood, went to him and conversed with him. The [jail] keeper was informed to whom Job belonged and what was the cause of his leaving his master. The keeper thereupon wrote to his master, who soon after fetched him home and was much kinder to him than before . . . [Job] wrote a letter in Arabic to his father, acquainting him with his misfortunes, hoping he might yet find means to redeem him. . . . It happened that this letter was seen by James Oglethorpe [a wealthy philanthropist and founder of the colony of Georgia], who . . . took compassion on Job and gave his bond . . . [for] delivery of Job here in England. . . .

In March 1733, he set sail in the *William* . . . in which ship I was also a passenger. . . . [We taught] him as much of the English language as we could . . .

On our arrival in England, we heard that Mr. Oglethorpe was gone to Georgia and that Mr. Hunt had provided a lodging for Job at Lime House. After I had visited my friends in the country, I went up on purpose to see Job. He was very sorrowful, and told me that Mr. Hunt had been applied to by some persons to sell him, who pretended they would send him home, but he feared they would either sell him again as a slave or if they sent him home would expect an unreasonable ransom for him. I took him to London with me and waited on Mr. Hunt to desire leave to carry him to Cheshunt in Hartfordshire . . .

Job, while he was at Cheshunt, had the honor to be sent for by most of the gentry of that place, who were mightily pleased with his company and concerned for his misfortunes. They made him several handsome presents and proposed that a subscription should be made for the payment of the money to Mr. Hunt. [Subsequently, several persons contributed funds to free him.]

[It was arranged] that Job should be accommodated at the African House [headquarters of the Royal African Company in London] at the Company's expense till one of the Company's ships should go to Gambia, in which he should be sent back to his friends without any ransom. The Company . . . asked me if they could do anything more to make Job easy, and upon my desire they ordered that Mr. Oglethorpe's bond should be canceled . . . and that Job should have his freedom in [writing]. . . . Job's mind being now perfectly easy . . . he went cheerfully among his friends to several places, both in town and country. One day . . . he expressed his great desire to see the Royal Family. . . . [H]e was soon clothed in a rich silk dress made up after his own country fashion, and introduced to their Majesties and the rest of the Royal Family. . . .

About the latter end of July last [1734], he embarked on board one of the African Company's ships bound for Gambia . . . [which arrived at the Gambia River in September]. On Job's first arrival here, he desired I would send a messenger up to his own country to acquaint his friends of his arrival. I spoke to one of the blacks which we usually employ upon those occasions, to procure me a messenger, who brought to me a Fulbe, who knew the High Priest, his father, and Job himself, and expressed great joy at seeing him in safety returned from slavery, he being the only man (except one) that was ever known to come back to this country after having been once carried a slave out of it by white men. Job gave him the message himself, and . . . sent some presents by him to his wives . . .

On the 14th [of February] a messenger, whom I had sent to Job's country, returned hither with letters and [news] that Job's father died before he got up thither, but that he had lived to receive the letters sent by Job from England, which brought him the welcome news of his son's being redeemed out of slavery and the figure he made in England; that one of Job's wives was married to another man, but that as soon as the husband heard of Job's arrival here he thought it advisable to abscond; that since Job's absence from this country there has been such a dreadful war that there is not so much as one cow left in it . . . [H]e wept grievously for his father's death and the misfortunes of his country. He forgave his wife and the man that had taken her, for . . . "she could not help thinking I was dead, for I was gone to a land from whence no Fulbe ever yet returned . . . "

On the 8th [of April, 1735], . . . I embarked on board the Company's sloop *James* . . . Job . . . came down with me to the sloop and parted with me with tears in his eyes, [and gave] me letters for his Grace the Duke of Montague, the Royal African Company, Mr. Oglethorpe, and several other gentlemen in England, telling me to . . . acquaint them that as he designs to learn to write the English tongue, he will, when he is master of it, send . . . full accounts of what shall happen to him hereafter . . .

Document 5
European Merchant Buying Slaves on the Slave Coast, 1702

Willem Bosman (1672–1702) worked for the Dutch West India Company on the Guinea Coast from 1688 until his death in 1702 at the age of thirty. As a factor (manager) of a trading station on the Slave Coast, he was well informed about the slave trade, and he related his observations in a series of letters to a relative in Holland, intending to publish them at a later date. However, information concerning overseas commercial ventures was considered a trade secret, and authorities imposed severe penalties for breaches of confidentiality. Therefore, Bosman's family did not publish his letters until after his death. In his book, later translated from Dutch into French and English, he describes various aspects of the purchase and treatment of slaves on the so-called Slave Coast in today's Benin, and refers specifically to the trading port of Ouidah and the neighboring state of Aja (Ardra). Reprinted by permission from Frank Cass and Co. Ltd. From Willem Bosman, *A New and Accurate Description of the Coast of Guinea* (1704; reprint, London: Frank Cass, 1967, 4th edition), 363–65.

The first business of one of our factors when he comes to Ouidah is to satisfy the customs [duties paid] to the king and the great men, which amounts to about 100 pounds in Guinea value . . . after which we have free license to trade . . . But yet before we can deal with any person, we are obliged to buy the king's whole stock of slaves at a set price, which is commonly one-third or one-fourth higher than ordinary. After [that] we obtain free leave to deal with all his subjects of . . . [any] rank. . . .

Not a few in our country fondly imagine that parents here sell their children, men their wives, and one brother the other, but those who think so deceive themselves for this never happens on any other account but that of necessity or some great crime. . . . Most of the slaves that are offered to us are prisoners of war, which are sold by the victors as their booty.

When these slaves come to Ouidah, they are put in prison all together, and when we negotiate their sale, they are all brought out together in a large plain where . . . they are thoroughly examined by our surgeons, even to the smallest member, both men and women naked without the least distinction or modesty. Those approved as good are set on one side, and the lame and faulty are set by as invalids, which are here called macrons. These [include those who] are above five and thirty years old or are maimed in the arms, legs, hands, or feet, have lost a tooth, are gray-haired, or have films over their eyes, as well as all those which are affected with any . . . distemper or with several other diseases.

The invalids and the maimed being removed, . . . the remainder are numbered, and it is entered [recorded] who delivered them. Meanwhile a burning iron, with the [coat of] arms or name of the companies, lies in the fire with which ours are marked on the breast. This is done that we may distinguish them from the slaves of the English, French, or others, . . . and to prevent the Negroes exchanging them for worse . . . I doubt not but this trade seems very barbarous to you, but since it is followed by mere necessity it must go on; but we yet take all possible care that they are not burned too hard, especially the women, who are more tender than the men.

We are seldom long detained in the buying of these slaves because their price is established, the women being one-fourth or -fifth part cheaper than the men. The disputes which we generally have with the owners of these slaves are that we will not give them such goods as they ask for them, especially the cowry shells (. . . the money of this country) of which they are very fond, though we generally [give an assortment of goods] . . . because those slaves which are paid for in cowries cost the company one-half more than those bought with other goods. . . .

You would really wonder to see how these slaves live on board, for though their number sometimes amounts to six or seven hundred, yet by the careful management of our masters of ships they are so regulated that it seems incredible. And in this particular our nation exceeds all other Europeans; for as the French, Portuguese, and English slave-ships are always foul and stinking, on the contrary ours are for the most part clean and neat.

The slaves are fed three times a day with [various] good victuals, ... Their lodging-place is divided into two parts, one of which is appointed for the men the other for the women, each sex being kept apart. Here they lie as close together as is possible . . .

We are sometimes . . . plagued with a parcel of slaves . . . from a far inland country who very innocently persuade one another that we buy them only to fatten and afterwards eat them as a delicacy. [On occasion] they resolve . . . to run away from the ship, kill the Europeans, and set the vessel ashore . . . to free themselves from being our food.

I have twice met with this misfortune . . . but the uproar was timely quashed by the master of the ship and myself by causing the abettor to be shot through the head, after which all was quiet.

But the second time . . . the male slaves . . . unknown to any of the ship's crew, possessed themselves of a hammer, with which in a short time they broke all their fetters . . . [and] came above deck and fell upon our men, some of whom they grievously wounded. [The slaves] would certainly have mastered the ship if a French and English ship had not very fortunately happened to lie by us [and, hearing] our distress gun . . . came to our assistance . . . About twenty [slaves] were killed. The Portuguese have been more unlucky in this particular than we, for in four years time they lost four ships in this manner.

Document 6
The Middle Passage from the Perspective of a Slave, 1750s

The following selection is a rare account of the experience aboard a slave ship during the Atlantic crossing from the perspective of a slave. It is a sequence to Olaudah Equiano's story of his enslavement in Africa (see document 1). This selection, written during the 1780s, describes his experience on the Middle Passage during the mid-1750s. Reprinted by permission from Harcourt Publishers. From Paul Edwards, ed., *Equiano's Travels* (Oxford: Harcourt, 1996), 22–27.

The first object which saluted my eyes when I arrived on the coast was the sea, and a slave ship which was then riding at anchor and waiting for its cargo. These filled me with astonishment, which was soon converted into terror when I was carried on board. I was immediately handled and tossed up to see if I were sound by some of the crew, and I was now persuaded that I had gotten into a world of bad spirits and that they were going to kill me. . . . Indeed such were the horrors of my views and fears at the moment that, if ten thousand worlds had been my own, I would have freely parted with them all to have exchanged my condition with that of the meanest slave in my own country. When I looked round the ship, too, and saw a large furnace or copper boiling and a multitude of black people of every description chained together, every one of their countenances expressing dejection and sorrow, I no longer doubted of my fate and . . . fainted. When I recovered a little I found some black people about me, who I believed were some of those who had brought me on board and had been receiving their pay; they talked to me in order to cheer me, but all in vain. I asked them if we were not to be eaten by those white men with horrible looks, red faces, and loose hair. They told me I was not, and one of the crew brought me a small portion of spirituous liquor in a wine glass, but being afraid of him I would not take it . . . Soon after this the blacks who brought me on board went off and left me abandoned to despair.

I now saw myself deprived of all chance of returning to my native country or even the least glimpse of hope of gaining the shore . . . and I even wished for my former slavery in preference to my present situation . . . I was soon put down under the decks, and there I received such a salutation in my nostrils as I had never experienced in my life; so that with the loathsomeness of the stench and crying together, I became so sick and low that I was not able to eat, nor had I the least desire to taste anything. . . . [T]wo of the white men offered me eatables, and on my refusing to eat, one of them held me fast by the hands and laid me across I think the windlass, and tied my feet while the other flogged me severely. I had never experienced anything of this kind before, and although, not being used to the water, I naturally feared that element the first time I saw it, yet nevertheless could I have got over the nettings I would . . . have jumped over the side . . . In a little time after, amongst the poor chained men I found some of my own nation, which in a small degree gave ease to my mind. I inquired of these what was to be done with us. [T]hey gave me to understand we were to be carried to these white people's country to work for them. I then was a little revived, and thought if it were no worse than working, my situation was not so desperate. But still I feared I should be put to death, the white people looked and acted, as I thought, in so savage a manner, for I had never seen among my people such instances of brutal cruelty, and this not only shown towards us blacks but also to some of the whites themselves. One white man in particular I saw . . . flogged so unmercifully with a large rope near the foremast that he died in consequence of it; and they tossed him over the side as they would have done a brute. This made me fear these people the more, and I expected nothing less than to be treated in the same manner.

I could not help expressing my fears and apprehensions to some of my countrymen. I asked them if these people had no country but lived in this hollow place (the ship). They told me they did not, but came from a distant one. "Then," said I, "how comes it in all our country we never heard of them?" They told me because they lived so very far off. . . . I asked how the vessel could go? They told me . . . there were cloths put upon the masts by the help of the ropes I saw . . . the white men had some spell or magic they put in the water when they liked in order to stop the vessel. I was exceedingly amazed at this account and really thought they were spirits. . . .

While we stayed on the coast I was mostly on deck, and one day . . . I saw one of these vessels coming in with the sails up. As soon as the whites saw it they gave a great shout, at which we were amazed, and the more so as the vessel appeared larger by approaching nearer. . . . [W]hen the anchor was let go, I and my countrymen who saw it were lost in astonishment to observe the vessel stop, and were now convinced it was done by magic. Soon after this the other ship got her boats out, and they came on board of us, and the people of both ships seemed very glad to see each other. Several of the strangers also shook hands with us black people, and made motions with their hands, signifying I suppose we were to go to their country; but we did not understand them. At last, when the ship we were in had got in all her cargo, they made ready with many fearful noises, and we were all put under deck so that we could not see how they managed the vessel. . . .

The stench of the hold while we were on the coast was so intolerably loathsome that it was dangerous to remain there for any time, and some of us had been permitted to stay on the deck for the fresh air. But now that the whole ship's cargo were confined together it became absolutely pestilential. The closeness of the place and the heat of the climate, added to the number in the ship, which was so crowded that each had scarcely room to turn himself, almost suffocated us. This produced copious perspiration, so that the air soon became unfit for respiration from a variety of loathsome smells and brought on a sickness among the slaves, of which many died . . . This wretched situation was again aggravated by the galling of the chains, now become insupportable, and the filth of the necessary tubs, into which the children often fell and were almost suffocated. The shrieks of the women and the groans of the dying rendered the whole a scene of horror almost inconceivable. Happily perhaps for myself, I was soon reduced so low here that it was thought necessary to keep me almost always on deck, and from my extreme youth I was not put in fetters. In this situation I expected every hour to share the fate of my companions, some of whom were almost daily brought upon deck at the point of death, which I began to hope would soon put an end to my miseries. . . .

One day they had taken a number of fishes, and when they had killed and satisfied themselves with as many as they thought fit, to our astonishment who were on the deck, rather than give any of them to us to eat as we expected, they tossed the remaining fish into the sea again, although we begged and prayed for some as well as we could, but in vain. And some of my countrymen, being pressed by hunger, took an opportunity when they thought no one saw them of trying to get a little privately; but they were discovered, and the attempt procured them some very severe floggings. One day, when we had a smooth sea and moderate wind, two of my wearied countrymen who were chained together . . . preferring death to such a life of misery, somehow made through the nettings and jumped into the sea. Immediately another quite dejected fellow, who on account of his illness was suffered to be out of irons, also followed their example. And I believe many more would very soon have done the same if they had not been prevented by the ship's crew, who were instantly alarmed. . . . Two of the wretches were drowned, but they got the other and afterwards flogged him unmercifully for thus attempting to prefer death to slavery.

In this manner we continued to undergo more hardships . . . Many a time we were near suffocation from the want of fresh air, which we were often without for whole days together. This and the stench of the necessary tubs carried off many. During our passage I first saw flying fishes, which surprised me very much. They used frequently to fly across the ship and many of them fell on the deck. I also now first saw the use of the quadrant. I had often with astonishment seen the mariners make observations with it, and I could not think what it meant. They at last took notice of my surprise, and one of them, willing to increase it as well as to gratify my curiosity, made me one day look through it . . .

Document 7
John Newton: From Slave Trader to Abolitionist, 1788

As the master's mate of one, and master of two transatlantic slaving expeditions and later a leading figure in the English abolitionist cause, John Newton knew the human traffic from both perspectives (see biographical sketch). The journals of his slave expeditions have been preserved and published. The following description of the evils of the slave trade and arguments for abolishing it were written more than thirty years after his involvement in the commerce but while it still flourished. *Source:* John Newton, "Thoughts upon the African Slave Trade," in *The Works of the Rev. John Newton*, vol. 6 (New York: Samuel Whiting and Co., 1811), 517–46.

I hope it will always be a subject of humiliating reflection to me that I was once an active instrument in a business at which my heart now shudders. . . . The slave trade was always unjustifiable; but inattention and interest prevented, for a time, the evil from being perceived. It is otherwise at present; the mischiefs and evils connected with it have been, of late years, represented with such undeniable evidence, and are now so generally known that I suppose . . . hardly an objection can be made to the wish of thousands, perhaps of millions, for the suppression of this trade, but upon the ground of political expedience. . . .

For the sake of method, I could wish to consider the African trade, first, with regard to the effect it has upon our own people, and secondly as it concerns the blacks . . . But these two topics are so interwoven together that it will not be easy to keep them exactly separate. . . .

The first point I shall mention is surely of political importance, if the lives of our fellow-subjects be so and if a rapid loss of seamen deserves the attention of a maritime people. This loss in the African trade is truly alarming. I admit that many [sailors] are cut off in their first voyage . . . before they can properly rank as seamen . . . [T]he neighborhood of our seaports is continually drained of men and boys to supply the places of those who die abroad, and if they are not all seamen they are all our brethren and countrymen. . . .

The sailors must be much exposed to the weather; especially on the Windward coast, where a great part of the cargo is procured by boats, which are often sent to the distance of thirty or forty leagues [90 to 120 miles], and are sometimes a month before they return. Many vessels arrive upon the coast before the rainy season, which continues from about May to October . . . and if trade be scarce, the ships which arrive in the fair or dry season often remain till the rains return, before they can complete their purchase. A proper shelter from the weather in an open boat, when the rain is incessant, night and day, for weeks and months, is impracticable.

I have, myself, in such a boat, been five or six days together, without . . . a dry thread about me. . . . And during the fair season, tornadoes or violent storms of wind, thunder, and heavy rain are very frequent, though they seldom last long. In fact, the boats seldom return without bringing some of the people ill of dangerous fevers or fluxes [dysentery], occasioned either by the weather or by unwholesome diet . . .

Strong liquors such as brandy, rum, or English spirits, the sailors cannot often procure in such quantities as to hurt them. But they will if they can, . . . for strong liquor being an article much in demand . . . is always at hand. . . . The article of women, likewise, contributes largely to the loss of our seamen. When they are on shore, they often . . . involve themselves on this account in quarrels with the natives, and if not killed upon the spot [they] are frequently poisoned.

The risk of insurrections is to be added. These, I believe, are always meditated, for the men slaves are not easily reconciled to their confinement and treatment; and if attempted they are seldom suppressed without considerable loss. And sometimes they succeed to the destruction of a whole ship's company at once. Seldom a year passes but we hear of one or more such catastrophes; and we likewise hear sometimes of whites and blacks involved, in one moment, in one common ruin, by the gunpowder taking fire and blowing up the ship. . . .

There is a . . . dreadful effect of this trade upon the minds of those who are engaged in it. . . . I know of no method of getting money . . . which has so direct a tendency to efface the moral sense, to rob the heart of every gentle and humane disposition and to harden it like steel, against all impressions of sensibility.

Usually, about two-thirds of a cargo of slaves are males. When a hundred and fifty or two hundred stout men, torn from their native land, many of whom never saw the sea much less a ship, till a short space before they had embarked. . . . who have probably the same natural prejudice against a white man as we have against a black, and who often bring with them an apprehension they are bought to be eaten. . . . When thus circumstanced, it is not to be expected that they will tamely resign themselves to their situation. It is always taken for granted that they will attempt to gain their liberty if possible. Accordingly, as we dare not trust them, we receive them on board from the first as enemies; and before their number exceeds . . . ten or fifteen, they are all put in irons; in most ships two and two together. And frequently, they are not thus confined. . . . as they might most conveniently stand or move, the right hand and foot of one to the left of the other, but across; that is, the hand and foot of each on the same side . . . are fettered together, so that they cannot move either hand or foot, but with great caution and with perfect consent. Thus they must sit, walk, and lie, for many months (sometimes for nine or ten), without any mitigation or relief, unless they are sick.

In the night, they are confined below. In the daytime (if the weather be fine) they are upon deck; and as they are brought by pairs, a chain is put through a ring upon their irons and this likewise locked down to the ring-bolts, which are fastened at certain intervals upon the deck. These . . . precautions are . . . necessary; especially as while the number of slaves increases [and] the people who are to guard them is diminished by sickness or death, or by being absent in the boats. . . . sometimes, not ten men can be mustered to watch night and day over two hundred . . .

One unguarded hour or minute is sufficient to give the slaves the opportunity they are always waiting for. An attempt to rise upon the ship's company brings on instantaneous and horrid war. For when they are once in motion, they are desperate; and where they do not conquer, they are seldom quelled without much mischief and bloodshed on both sides.

Sometimes, when the slaves are ripe for an insurrection, one of them will impeach [betray] the affair . . . The traitor to the cause of liberty is caressed, rewarded, and deemed an honest fellow. The patriots, who formed and animated the plan, if they can be found out, must be treated as villains and punished to intimidate the rest. These punishments . . . depend upon the sovereign will of the captain. Some are content with inflicting such moderate punishment as may suffice for an example. But unlimited power—instigated by revenge and where the heart by a long familiarity with the sufferings of slaves is become callous and insensible to the pleadings of humanity—is terrible!

I have seen them sentenced to unmerciful whippings, continued till the poor creatures have not had power to groan under their misery, and hardly a sign of life has remained. I have seen them agonizing for hours, I believe for days . . . under the torture of the thumbscrews; a dreadful engine, which, if the screw be turned by an unrelenting hand, can give intolerable anguish. . . .

Hitherto, I have considered the condition of the men slaves only. From the women, there is no danger of insurrection and they are carefully kept from the men. . . . When the women and girls are taken on board a ship, naked, trembling, terrified, perhaps almost exhausted with cold, fatigue, and hunger, they are often exposed to the wanton rudeness of white savages. The poor creatures cannot understand the language they hear, but the looks and manner of the speakers are sufficiently intelligible. In imagination the prey is divided upon the spot, and only reserved till opportunity offers. Where resistance or refusal would be utterly in vain, even the solicitation of consent is seldom thought of. . . .

Perhaps some hard-hearted pleader may suggest that . . . "African women are savages" . . . I dare contradict them in the strongest terms. I have lived long and conversed much amongst these supposed savages. I have often slept in their towns, in a house filled with goods for trade, with no person in the house but myself and with no other door than a mat, in that security which no man in his senses would expect in this civilized nation, especially in this metropolis, without the precaution of having strong doors strongly locked and bolted. . . .

And with regard to the women in Sherbro, where I was most acquainted, I have seen many instances of modesty and even delicacy which would not disgrace an English woman. Yet, such is the treatment which I have known permitted, if not encouraged, in many of our ships, they have been abandoned without restraint to the lawless will of the first comer.

Accustomed thus to despise, insult, and injure the slaves on board, it may be expected that the conduct of many of our people to the natives with whom they trade is, as far as circumstances admit, very similar. . . . They are considered as a people to be robbed and spoiled with impunity. Every art is employed to deceive and wrong them. . . .

The natives are cheated, in the number, weight, measure, or quality of what they purchase, in every possible way. And by habit and emulation a marvelous dexterity is acquired in these practices. And thus the natives in their turn, in proportion to their commerce with the Europeans, . . . They know with whom they deal and are accordingly prepared, though they can trust some ships and boats which have treated them with punctuality and may be trusted by them. A quarrel sometimes furnishes pretext for detaining and carrying away one or more of the natives, which is retaliated . . . upon the next boat that comes to the place from the same port. . . .

Retaliation on their parts furnishes a plea for reprisal on ours. Thus, in one place or another, trade is often suspended, all intercourse cut off, and things are in a state of war till necessity, either on the ship's part or on theirs, produces overtures of peace and dictates the price which the offending party must pay for it. But it is a warlike peace . . . For, with a few exceptions, the English and the Africans, reciprocally, consider each other as consummate villains, who are always watching opportunities to do mischief. In short, we have, I fear too deservedly, a very unfavorable character [reputation] on the coast. When I have charged a black with unfairness and dishonesty, he has answered, if able to clear himself, with an air of disdain, "What! Do you think I am a white man?"

Such is the nature, such are the concomitants of the slave trade; and such is the school in which many thousands of our seamen are brought up. Can we, then wonder at that impatience of subordination and that disposition to mutiny amongst them, which has been of late so loudly complained of, and so severely felt? . . .

With our ships, the great object is to be full. When the ship is there, it is thought desirable she should take as many [slaves] as possible. The cargo of a vessel of a hundred tons . . . is calculated to purchase from two hundred and twenty to two hundred and fifty slaves. Their lodging rooms below the deck, which are three (for the men, the boys, and the women), besides a place for the sick, are sometimes no more than five feet high, and sometimes less. And this height is divided towards the middle, for the slaves lie in two rows, one above the other, on each side of the ship, close to each other like books upon a shelf. I have known them so close that the shelf would not easily contain one more. And I have known a white man sent down among the men to lay them in these rows to the greatest advantage, so that as little space as possible might be lost.

Let it be observed that the poor creatures, thus cramped for want of room, are likewise in irons, for the most part both hands and feet, and two together, which makes it difficult for them to turn or move, to attempt either to rise or to lie down, without hurting themselves or each other. Nor is the motion of the ship . . . when under sail to be omitted; for . . . as they lie athwart, or cross the ship, adds to the uncomfortableness of their lodging, especially to those who lie on the leeward or leaning side of the vessel. . . .

The heat and smell of these rooms, when the weather will not admit of the slaves being brought upon deck and of having their rooms cleaned every day, would be almost insupportable to a person not accustomed to them. . . . They are kept down by the weather to breathe a hot and corrupted air, sometimes for a week. This, added to the galling of their irons and the despondency which seizes their spirits when thus confined, soon becomes fatal. And every morning, perhaps more instances than one are found of the living and the dead . . . fastened together.

Epidemic fevers and fluxes, which fill the ship with noisome and noxious effluvia, often break out and infect the seamen likewise; and thus the oppressors and the oppressed fall by the same stroke. I believe nearly one-half of the slaves on board have sometimes died, and that the loss of a third part in these circumstances is not unusual. . . .

I . . . write from memory after an interval of more than thirty years. But at the same time, I believe [that] many things which I saw, heard, and felt upon the coast of Africa are so deeply engraved in my memory that I can hardly forget or greatly mistake them . . . I am certainly not guilty of wilful misrepresentation . . . I dare appeal to the Great Searcher of hearts, in whose presence I write, and before whom I and my readers must all shortly appear, that (with the restrictions and exceptions I have made) I have advanced nothing but what, to the best of my judgement and conscience, is true. . . .

Document 8
Guidelines for the Slave Trade at Ouidah on the Slave Coast

The following document was written by the Dutch factor Willem Bosman in 1700, as a guide for Dutch slave traders at the port of

Ouidah. At that time, he was stationed at Elmina as second in command of the West India Company's establishment on the Guinea Coast. During the previous decade he had been stationed as a factor in Ouidah, and had become quite familiar with the slave trade in that region. Reprinted with permission from Cambridge University Press. From Johannes Postma, *The Dutch in the Atlantic Slave Trade, 1600–1815* (New York: Cambridge University Press, 1990), 363–65.

Guidelines according to which one may regulate the slave trade at Ouidah. Composed by the Honorable Chief Factor Willem Bosman, and currently used by the Chief Commissioner Nicolaas Pol. . . .

1. On arrival, the captain [of the ship] must make certain that he gives generous presents to the king, and in addition pay the required duties, which are:

To the King—six slaves, paid in cowries, plus two slaves for water;
To the Chiefs [principal traders]—two slaves for each;
To the Announcer—one pitcher of cowries, when he announces the free market.

2. When the duties have been paid and the market announced, the captain is still not allowed to buy slaves until he has negotiated with the king first. After that he is free to trade with any merchant. Try to buy the fewest possible slaves from the king, since he always demands cowries as payment—approximately 120 pounds per slave. Although a captain cannot avoid buying a sizable number from the king, he may terminate [the process] when prices get too high.

3. To the three or four merchants [captains or chiefs] who furnish the largest number of slaves, the same price is calculated as with the king, but it is paid in [European] merchandise, and not in cowries, at a rate of about 1/8, 1/5, or 1/6 more than to private traders. . . . For a woman one generally pays one piece of any kind of merchandise less [than for a man]. Cowries have a stable price. . . . As a rule we also pay the Negro Assoe a little more, and because he is of great service to us and sells us many slaves we give him cowries as a reward—to the value of a slave.

4. If one trades with the English factor, the price of 95 pounds of cowries [per slave] is the rule; and if paid in goods, the same price counts as with the king and the chief merchants. If the captain wants to verify price levels, which continually fluctuate, the best thing to do is to

see either the [following Africans] Negro Assoe, Captain Carte, or the interpreter Agay. The reliability of these Negroes need not be questioned. These men can also supply information regarding the charges for transporting merchandise. For these reasons it is important that ship captains remain on good terms with these persons.

5. Captains should carefully watch out for the thievery of the Negroes, in order that not too much gets stolen. I say "too much," since it is almost impossible to escape theft completely; at least I have never heard of such a situation. Even the rowers hired by the captain will try to steal. For this reason he must watch everyone, since theft seems to be an inherited trait of the people there.

6. The captain should try, if possible, to sell his [European] merchandise first and keep his cowries, otherwise the slave prices will increase too much. When the trade stagnates, no improvement can be effected without the use of cowries, and he should act as seems best for the Honorable [West India] Company, since keeping [a ship] on the coast for a long time is most disadvantageous. . . .

7. Finally, when trading has been completed, the following customs should be paid—again in cowries: [the value of] one slave for lodging [stockade]; one slave to the interpreter; one slave for those who have taken the slaves to the beach; one slave for those who have taken the merchandise from the beach to the lodge; and one to the wives of the king. From the latter we gain the following advantage. If a few slaves escape from their stockade or during transport to the beach, the king will recapture them or compensate us. One should not always count on this, however.

Also, the gifts to the king's wives cover the daily supplies for the table, making this actually the best investment. Finally, before one leaves, it is customary to make another present to the king, and also to the principal traders who have supplied large numbers of slaves. These, in addition to the daily supplies of brandy, are the expenses of the captain. If greater expenditures are demanded, he can reply that such is against the established customs and that he has no desire to introduce new practices. . . .

Document 9
A Slave Trade Contract for the *Asiento* Trade with Spanish America

Because Spain did not have trading stations in Africa, they relied on other European nations to bring slaves to their American colonies. At first, Portugal shipped slaves to the Spanish colonies, but the Dutch gained control of this market by the middle of the seventeenth century. Then the French briefly supplied the Spanish colonies before British carriers acquired the contract (the *asiento*) with the Spanish government in 1713. The following are excerpts from a 1667 contract spelling out the terms of the agreement with Dutch shippers. The unsigned, handwritten document was probably a draft from which the official contract was copied. Reprinted with permission from Cambridge University Press. From Johannes Postma, *The Dutch in the Atlantic Slave Trade, 1600–1815* (New York: Cambridge University Press, 1990), 349–53.

In the name of the Lord, Amen. In the year of our merciful Lord Jesus Christ [1667], on the 16th of May, appeared before me, Pieter Padthuysen, public notary for the Court of Holland, resident of Amsterdam, in the presence of the following witnesses: . . .

The directors of the WIC [West India Company] . . . as the first party of this [contract], and the other—Mr. Francisco Ferony, merchant in this city, as representative of Messrs. Domingo Grillo and Ambrosio Lomelin, residing at Madrid, Spain. . . .

I confirm that the individuals mentioned have agreed with each other on the following contract: that the respective directors of the WIC shall dispatch from time to time an adequate number of ships and cargoes to the coast of Africa and purchase there a total of 4,000 deliverable [acceptable] slaves, to wit pieces of India, and deliver these during the current year 1667 and before the end of December 1668, at the island of Curaçao to the agents of the mentioned Grillo and Lomelin. When these 4,000 Negroes have been handed over . . . they will be paid for as stipulated below, and in addition to the 4,000 Negroes the WIC directors will be allowed an additional 500 on the same conditions and for the same price as the 4,000 Negroes.

None of the aforementioned slaves may be obtained from the areas of Calabar, Del Rey, or the Cameroons, and all those that are without major blemish, who are in good health, not blind, lame, or broken, will be counted as deliverable.

The following stipulation shall be made in respect to their age. Those between the ages of 15 and 36 will be counted as deliverable, [valid] pieces of India; those from the age of 8 to 15 and 36 to 42 will be counted as three persons for two pieces of India; those below 8 and down to 4 years of age will be counted as two persons for one piece of India; those below the age of four will remain with their mothers.

In respect to the gender ratios, two-thirds of the slaves delivered must be male persons, and the remaining one-third portion shall be women. Messrs. Grillo and Lomelin will not be obligated to take any more than one-third women slaves. If, however, the [WIC] directors deliver more than two-thirds male slaves, they will be paid for at a rate of seven pesos (pieces of eight) per piece of India more than the regular contracted number.

. . . Messrs. Grillo and Lomelin must keep well-stocked factories on the island of Curaçao for the reception and payment of contracted slaves. The factors must examine newly arrived shipments of slaves within a period of 14 days and separate the deliverable from the undeliverable. After this is done, the WIC directors will be responsible for the maintenance of the deliverable Negroes for an additional 24 days, or a total of 38 days after the arrival of each ship, for both risk and maintenance . . .

After the waiting period of three months has expired without any payment being received for the separated deliverable slaves, the WIC directors may feel free to dispose of the slaves to their best advantage, instead of keeping them any longer for Messrs. Grillo and Lomelin . . .

While the separated slaves are being held at Curaçao the WIC directors are entitled to put the Negroes to work for the profit of the company. It is advisable that this would lead to a slight reduction of the maintenance cost charged to Messrs. Grillo and Lomelin. Once the maintenance fees have been paid, the WIC is obligated to deliver the slaves immediately.

Messrs. Grillo and Lomelin commit themselves to pay for each "deliverable piece Negro of India," at the time of transfer, 107 ½ quality pieces of eight. This payment exempts Messrs. Grillo and Lomelin from any fees or duties that [the Nineteen] directors of the WIC would ordinarily demand for the sale of slaves . . .

The WIC directors must instruct the Assistant Director at Curaçao to receive and treat the factors of Messrs. Grillo and Lomelin with the greatest courtesy and assist them (and also in Amsterdam) in every way necessary to carry out their duties and to maintain order and authority over their employees. To assist them to this end is required by civilized standards, and it should contribute to good relations and friendship between the contracting parties.

Finally, the contracting parties agree that the mentioned Mr. Ferony, as representative of Messrs. Grillo and Lomelin, shall pay to the directors of the WIC the sum of 6,000 Caroli guilders, in rough silver, immediately after the signing of this document . . .

In confirmation of these agreements the parties involved, namely the WIC directors, commit all the effects and means of the mentioned company, and Mr. Ferony with power of attorney for Messrs. Grillo and Lomelin, commit all their personal effects and means, placing themselves before all courts and justices in good faith. Agreed upon in Amsterdam, in the presence of requested witnesses . . .

Document 10
Slave Revolt Aboard the *Little George*, 1730

Africans often resisted their enslavement and tried to escape from the slave ships. Their resistance took various forms; refusing to eat and jumping overboard were not uncommon, and collective rebellions were also frequently organized. The following testimony of the captain of an American slave ship describes a revolt that took place off the coast of Sierra Leone in 1730. Although most revolts failed, this one was quite successful. The captain's dramatic account is, of course, from his perspective. Reprinted with permission from the Carnegie Institution. From Elisabeth Donnan, *Documents Illustrative of the Slave Trade to America*, vol. 3 (Washington, D.C.: Carnegie Institution, 1930–35): 118–21.

I, George Scott, master of the sloop *Little George*, belonging to Rhode Island, sailed from the Banana Islands on the coast of Guinea, the first day of June, 1730, having on board ninety-six slaves (thirty-five of which were men). On the 6th of said Month, at half an hour past four of the Clock in the morning, being about 100 leagues [300 miles] distant from the land, the men slaves got off their Irons, and making way through the bulkhead of the Deck, killed the watch, consisting of John Harris Doctor, Jonathan Ebens Cooper, and Thomas Ham Sailor, who were . . . all asleep. I, being then in my Cabin and hearing a noise upon deck . . . took my pistol directly and fired up the scuttle [hatchway in the deck] . . . , which made all the slaves that were loose run forwards, except one or two men . . . who kept us . . . confined in the cabin, and passing by the companion to view us, we shot two men slaves.

On so sudden a surprise, we were at a loss what to do. But consulting together, [we] filled two round bottles with powder, put . . . fuses to them in order to send them among the slaves, with a design at the same instant of time to issue out upon them, and either suppress them or lose our lives. But just as we were putting our design in execution, one of the slaves let fall an Ax (either through accident or design) which broke the bottle as Thomas Dickinson was setting fire to the fuse. Taking fire with a keg of powder in the Cabin, raised up the deck, blew open the cabin doors and windows, discharged all our fire arms but one, destroyed our Cloths, and burnt the man that had the Bottle in his hand in a most miserable manner, and myself with the rest very much hurt thereby.

Upon this unhappy accident, we expected no less than immediate death, which would have been unavoidable had they at that juncture of time rushed in upon us. And being in this consternation and hopeless, [we] sent up the boy in order . . . to bring them to terms, but they slighted our message. And soon after . . . we found the other bottle of powder which, by providence, had not taken fire. [This] put new life and vigor into us, that we were resolved to withstand them to the uttermost, and accordingly loaded our arms and shot several of the slaves, which occasioned all the men slaves to betake themselves to the quarter deck . . . [above us]. The Slaves then got two swivel guns and filled them almost full with powder, which they found in the fore-hold as they were looking for provisions. [They] . . . designed to blow the bulkhead in upon us, which they put fire to several times but could not get off by reason of wet weather. We had two carriage guns in the boat, which we expected the slaves would get out, and therefore watched them very narrowly. But in a dark night they [got them] . . . and brought them upon the quarter deck, [where] they loaded one of the guns and pointed it directly down the scuttle. We hearing them . . . and having prepared ourselves, as soon as they lifted it up we shot the man dead that pointed the gun. Another . . . slave standing by [set] . . . a match to it and fired it off, which blew the scuttle all to pieces and some of the deck, but did us no damage. They then took pieces of boards and laid them over the scuttle and the hole they had made in the deck, and laid the Tarpaulin with a great weight upon them to prevent our coming up.

Then they made sail . . . towards land and were continually heaving down billets of wood and water into the Cabin, with [the] intention to disable us and spoil our small arms. [On] . . . the fourth day after the rising [they reached] . . . the same land we departed from, then stood off and on again for four or five days more, in which time the boy, being forced by hunger, ran up among the slaves, who immediately put him in irons. They made several attempts to come down into the cabin, but their courage failed them. I then called to them to come down to decide the matter, they answered by and by.

Finding ourselves grown very weak through these hardships and for want of sustenance, we thought it proper before our strength was quite spent to take some desperate course. I proposed to cut away the ceiling and bore some holes through the vessel's bottom, which . . . was directly done and let in about three feet of water. I then called to the slaves and told them I would drown them all, which frightened them exceedingly. They then sent the boy to the cabin door to tell us that they had but just made the land, and that when they got a little nearer the shore, they would take the boat and leave them with the young slaves. I told them if they would do that I would not sink [the ship]. (My design in letting the water in was to force the vessel on her side that we might get some advantage.) They stood in for the land about 12 o'clock at night [and] struck upon the [sand] bar of Sierra Leone River, and were in great danger of being lost. The vessel . . . beat over the bar, and they ran ashore about three leagues up the river, on the north side. [This] being then high Water, and by seven o'clock the next morning there was not above a foot of water alongside.

The natives waded from the shore with fire arms, would have tried to overcome us, but were persuaded from it by the slaves on board, who told them we would shoot them if they appeared in our sight. They persuaded the grown Slaves to go ashore and drove the young ones over board and then followed them, making the vessel shake at their departure. Our Boy assuring us the slaves had all left the vessel, we immediately went up with our Arms, and saw the slaves just ashore. We found our great guns loaded quite full. And as we hoisted out our boat, the natives mustered very thick on the shore and fired at us [several] times. We made what haste we could to the other side of the river, where we rowed down about two leagues and found a sloop riding in Frenchman's Bay belonging to Montserat [a Caribbean island], James Collingwood Commander, where we refreshed ourselves, being all of us in a weak and miserable condition, having had nothing to subsist upon during the Nine Days we were under this affliction but raw rice.

Document 11
Instructions for Slave Ship Captains, Eighteenth Century

The Middelburg Commercial Company in the Netherlands province of Zeeland gave formal instructions to the captains and crews of its slave ships concerning how they were to conduct themselves purchasing slaves, and how they would be compensated. The instructions were printed, but the name of the ship, destination, and additional directions were filled in by hand. Handwritten additions on this document are shown in italics. Reprinted with permission from Cambridge University Press. From Johannes Postma, *The Dutch in the Atlantic Slave Trade, 1600–1815* (New York: Cambridge University Press, 1990), 366–68.

Private instructions for captains and officers of the ship *De Nieuwe Hoop* of the Commercie Compagnie at Middelburg in Zeeland

---

I

According to article 3 of the General Instructions, you shall proceed with your voyage and as quickly as possible sail to the coast of Guinea in Africa; and after arriving there you must purchase, with the greatest care and most profitably, a high quality transport (*armazoen*) of slaves. After that, sail with the slaves to Surinam in America, according to instructions given in article 9 below. *Also, purchase as many ivory tusks as possible.*

II

As mentioned in article 4 of the General Instructions, precautions should be taken that you not be attacked by Negroes or slaves. We also seriously demand that you do not permit any Negroes, slaves, or slave women to be defiled or mistreated by any of the officers or crew members. And if such should occur anyway, it should be noted in the log book, a signed affidavit must be submitted, and the offender shall be punished by the ship's council in accordance with the offense, including confiscation of his salary.

III

Also, the person(s) in command shall see to it that the slaves are treated well, and properly inspected and cared for. Also, the "slave kettle" [large pot in which food was cooked] must be kept clean. *Likewise, care should be taken that the doctor and supercargo* [merchant in charge of the cargo] *check the mouths and eyes of the slaves every morning, and try to discover if anything ails them. The captain is obligated to supply the doctor with everything he needs for the slaves.*

IV

It is our fervent intent that neither you [captain] nor any of the officers bring along any merchandise, or privately buy and sell slaves. You are ordered once more to watch carefully that everyone obey this rule; and if you discover any violation of this rule, you must note this in the ship's log, and deal with the offender appropriately. Furthermore, you should involve the ship's council in obtaining evidence and a declaration, which will be of service to us after your return, and, in case you should die, would no longer be available. And even if such [private trade] is undertaken for reason of improving trading conditions, the directors will still not approve of it. Upon your return, you may be requested to declare, under oath, that neither you nor your officers had brought any merchandise or used this to trade in slaves; if this should turn out to be the case, the offender shall have his salary and premiums confiscated; in addition, he must pay a fine of 1,000 guilders for every slave, male or female, that he has traded; and such a person will forever be barred from serving this company, and he will legally be charged with perjury.

In return, the directors promise to pay you and all officers, upon your return, for every slave (male and female) landed and sold in the Americas, a premium as follows:

To the Captain	80 stuivers per slave [20 stuivers in a guilder]
To the First Mate	24 stuivers per slave
To the Second Mate	10 stuivers per slave
To the Third Mate	6 stuivers per slave
To the Supercargo	24 stuivers per slave
Total:	144 stuivers per slave

Everyone should be satisfied with this. *Similar amounts shall be paid for the ivory* [tusks] *as if slaves had been purchased.*

V

The premiums mentioned above have to be paid even if no more than the cost price is obtained for slaves and backhaul [goods returned from the Americas]. But if it turns out that, after all salaries and expenses for this ship and its cargo have been paid, a profit has been made, then, and only then, will the earlier mentioned officers receive an extra premium of 12 percent of the profits; no more, and only once for each of them. This [share of the] profit will be divided among them according to the ratio of the "slave money." And if, by some chance, the ship should experience some unusual disaster, the premium will be based on the profit still remaining.

VI

If it should happen that two or more ships of this company meet in the same colony where you sell slaves, the one that arrived first shall sell the slaves first and then continue its voyage as soon as possible. The second ship shall return the bills of exchange of both ships, unless these had been sent with another ship beforehand.

VII

The export of ammunition on your ship, allowed by the Admiralty [navy] Council here, is permitted on the following condition: that upon your return you can prove that the ammunition, as specified on the documents, has been taken ashore in Africa and stored there. You will be required to sign, along with your officers, a written declaration of this, in order that the company can account for it at the Admiralty Council.

VIII

As you purchase slaves you must mark them at the upper right arm with the silver marker CC N. which is sent along . . . Note the following when you do the branding: (1) The area of marking must first be rubbed with candle wax or oil; (2) The marker should be only as hot as when applied to paper, the paper gets red. When these [precautions] are observed, the slaves will not suffer bad effects from the branding.

Document 12
Equiano's Arrival and Sale in the Caribbean, 1750s

The following selection narrates Olaudah Equiano's experiences as he arrives at Barbados and is sold to a new owner in America. For his capture in Africa and experiences on the Middle Passage, see documents 1 and 6. Reprinted by permission from Harcourt Publishers. From Paul Edwards, ed., *Equiano's Travels* (Oxford: Harcourt, 1996), 27–31.

At last we came in sight of the island of Barbados, at which the whites on board gave a great shout and made many signs of joy to us. We did not know what to think of this, but as the vessel drew nearer we plainly saw the harbor and other ships of different kinds and sizes, and we soon anchored amongst them off Bridgetown. Many merchants and planters now came on board . . . They put us in separate parcels and examined us attentively. They also made us jump, and pointed to the land, signifying we were to go there. We thought by this we should be eaten by these ugly men . . . and when soon after we were all put down under the deck again, there was much dread and trembling among us, and nothing but bitter cries to be heard all the night from these apprehensions, insomuch that at last the white people got some old slaves from the land to pacify us. They told us we were not to be eaten but to work, and were soon to go on land where we should see many of our country people.

This report eased us much; and sure enough, soon after we were landed there came to us Africans of all languages. We were conducted immediately to the merchant's yard, where we were all pent up together like so many sheep in a fold without regard to sex or age. As every object was new to me everything I saw filled me with surprise. What struck me first was that the houses were built with storeys, and in every other respect different from those in Africa. But I was still more astonished on seeing people on horseback. I did not know what this could mean, and indeed I thought these people were full of nothing but magical arts. While I was in this astonishment, one of my fellow prisoners spoke to a countryman of his about the horses, who said they were the same kind they had in their country. I understood them, though they were from a distant part of Africa, and I thought it odd I had not seen any horses there . . .

We were not many days in the merchant's custody before we were sold after their usual manner, which is this: On a signal given (as the beat of a drum), the buyers rush at once into the yard where the slaves are confined and make choice of that parcel they like best. The noise and clamor with which this is attended and the eagerness visible in the countenances of the buyers serve not a little to increase the apprehensions of the terrified Africans . . .

In this manner, without scruple, are relations and friends separated, most of them never to see each other again. I remember in the vessel in which I was brought over, in the men's apartment there were several brothers who, in the sale, were sold in different lots; and it was very moving on this occasion to see and hear their cries at parting. . . .

I stayed in this island for . . . a fortnight when . . . we were shipped off in a sloop to North America. On the passage we were better treated than when we were coming from Africa, and we had plenty of rice and fat pork. We were landed up a river a good way from the sea, about Virginia county, where we saw few or none of our native Africans . . . I was a few weeks weeding grass and gathering stones in a plantation, and at last all my companions were distributed . . . I had no person to speak that I could understand. . . .

In this place I was called Jacob, but on board of the *African* now I was called Michael. I had been some time in this miserable . . . and much dejected state without having anyone to talk to . . . when . . . one day the captain of the merchant ship called the *Industrious Bee* came on some business to my master's house. This gentleman, whose name was Michael Henry Pascal, . . . commanded this trading ship. . . . While he was at my master's house it happened that he saw me and liked me so well that he made a purchase of me. I think I have often heard him say he gave thirty or forty pound sterling for me . . . [H]e meant me for a present to some of his friends in England, and I was sent accordingly . . . to the place where the ship lay . . . I was carried aboard a fine large ship, loaded with tobacco, etc., and just ready to sail for England. I now thought my condition much mended. I had sails to lie on and plenty of good victuals to eat, and everybody on board [treated me] very kindly, quite contrary to what I had seen of any white people before. I therefore began to think that they were not all of the same disposition.

Document 13
King Osei Bonsu's Reaction to Abolition, 1820

In 1820, twelve years after Britain ended its participation in the Atlantic slave trade, King Osei Bonsu of the Asante Kingdom (in today's Ghana) spoke through interpreters with Joseph Dupuis, who represented Britain's King George IV, about the effect of Britain's withdrawal from the slave trade. Reprinted with permission from Frank Cass and Co. Ltd. From Joseph Dupuis, *Journal of a Residence in Ashantee* (1824; reprint, London: Frank Cass, 1966, 2nd edition), 162–64.

"Now," said the [Asante] king after a pause, "I have another palaver [issue for discussion], and you must help me to talk it. A long time ago the great king [of England] liked plenty of trade, more than now; then many ships came and they bought ivory, gold, and slaves. But now he will not let the ships come as before, and the people buy gold and ivory only. This is what I have in my head, so now tell me truly, like a friend, why does the king do so?"

"His majesty's question," I replied, "was connected with a great palaver which my instructions did not authorize me to discuss. . . . " "I know that too," retorted the king, "because if my master liked that trade, you would have told me so before. I only want to hear what you think as a friend; this is not like the other palavers."

I was, confessedly, at a loss for an argument that might pass as a satisfactory reason, and the sequel proved that my doubts were not groundless. The king did not deem it plausible that this obnoxious traffic should have been abolished from motives of humanity alone, neither would he admit that it lessened the number of either domestic or foreign wars.

Taking up one of my observations, he remarked: "The white men who go to council with your master and pray to the great God for him do not understand my country or they would not say the slave trade was bad. But if they think it bad now, why did they think it good before? Is not your law an old law, the same as the . . . [Islamic] law? Do you not both serve the same God, only you have different fashions and customs? [Muslims] . . . are strong people in fetische[s] [protective spirits], and they say the law is good because the great God made the book [Quran]; so they buy slaves and teach them good things which they knew not before. This makes everybody love the . . . [Muslims] and they go everywhere up and down, and the people give them food when they want it. Then these men come all the way from the great water [Niger River], . . . they stop and trade for slaves and then go home. If the great king would like to restore this trade, it would be good for the white men and for me, too, because Asante is a country for war and the people are strong. So if you talk that palaver for me properly in the white country . . . I will give you plenty of gold, and I will make you richer than all the white men."

I urged the impossibility of the king's request, promising . . . to record his sentiments faithfully. "Well then," said the king, "you must put down in my master's book all I shall say, and then he will look to it, now [that] he is my friend. And when he sees what is true, he will surely restore that trade. I cannot make war to catch slaves in the bush like a thief. My ancestors never did so. But if I fight a king and kill him when he is insolent, then certainly I must have his gold and his slaves, and [his] people are mine too. Do not the white kings act like this? Because I hear the old men say that before I conquered Fantee [kingdom] and killed the Brassoes [chiefs] and the kings, white men came in great ships and fought and killed many people. And then they took the gold and slaves to the white country, and sometimes they fought . . . [It] is . . . the same in these black countries.

"The great God and the fetische[s] made war for strong men everywhere, because then they can pay plenty of gold and proper sacrifice. When I fought Gaman, I did not make war for slaves but because [the king of] Denkyira sent me an arrogant message and killed my people, and refused to pay me gold [tribute] as his father did. Then my fetische[s] made me strong like my ancestors, and I killed [the] Dinkera [king's title], and took his gold and brought more than 20,000 slaves to Kumasi [the Asante capital]. Some of these people being bad men, I washed my stool [three-footed seat; symbol of authority] in their blood for the fetische[s]. But then some were good people, and these I sold or gave to my captains. Many . . . died, however, because this country does not grow . . . much corn like Sarem [does], and what can

I do [about that]? Unless I kill or sell them, they will grow strong and kill my people. Now you must tell my master [the king of England] that these slaves can work for him, and if he wants 10,000 he can have them. And if he wants fine handsome girls and women to give his captains, I can send him great numbers."

GLOSSARY OF TERMS

Asiento. A contract with the Spanish government that entitled the other party monopoly rights to import a specified number of slaves into the Spanish American colonies.

Bozal. A newly arrived slave who was born in Africa.

Branding. The practice of burning a recognition mark on the skin.

Chattel slavery. The most severe form of slavery, where slaves were property that could be bought and sold, and their labor and sexuality were completely at the disposal of the master.

Coasting. A mobile method of obtaining slaves on the African coast. Ships moved from one place to another to purchase small numbers of slaves.

Coffle. A group of slaves tied together in single file and forced to march to a coastal destination, where they were sold and embarked on slave ships.

Creole (Criollo). A person of African descent born in the Americas. Creole is also used as an adjective for languages and other cultural features created by such persons.

Diaspora. The dispersal or forced emigration of Africans by means of the slave trade.

Domestic slave. In Africa, a slave who was part of a community and not intended to be sold as a trade slave. In the Americas, a slave used in the home rather than in the fields.

Emancipation. Freeing from slavery, generally as a group.

Encomienda.   Forced labor system or tax payment imposed on American Indians by their Spanish colonial rulers.

Illicit trade.   In connection with the slave trade, continued traffic in slaves after it had been prohibited by national law or international conventions.

Indenture.   A labor contract in which a person bound himself or herself to unlimited service for a specified number of years. The method was used to attract European laborers to the Americas during the sixteenth and seventeenth centuries.

Interlopers.   Ships that ventured into waters reserved for monopoly companies, sanctioned by government contracts.

Macron.   A newly arrived slave with physical or mental deficiencies, who did not qualify as a Pieza de (piece of) India. Macrons were usually auctioned off separately.

Manumission.   The freeing of an individual from the bonds of slavery.

Maroons.   Slaves who ran away and established themselves in communities through which they maintained their freedom and independence.

Mulatto.   A person with one white and one black parent.

Pieza de India.   A designation in Spanish, measuring a slave's potential labor value based primarily on age and physical condition. Children were often valued in fractions of a Pieza de India. The term originated with the slave trade to the Spanish colonies and was adopted by other nations that transported slaves there.

Scramble.   A method of selling newly arrived slaves in the West Indies, in which potential buyers would move among the slaves and lay claim to specific ones at a standard price. The auction or individual sale methods eventually became prevalent.

Serfdom.   A form of bondage practiced in the European Middle Ages, in which persons (serfs) belonged to the land on which they lived and owed labor services to the titleholder of the land.

Triangular trade.   Trade involving three linked routes and ports of destination in Africa, America, and Europe. The Atlantic slave trade is generally characterized as such, although the Brazilian traffic was bilateral. North Americans also used a triangular pattern by linking their home ports in America with Africa and the West Indies.

SELECT AND ANNOTATED BIBLIOGRAPHY

Books

The books listed below include both primary and secondary works. The list is far from exhaustive because much has been published on the subject of the slave trade in the past decades. Several of the books have been cited in the text or with the documents, but many additional publications have been added to assist with further research.

Anstey, Roger. *The Atlantic Slave Trade and British Abolition, 1760–1810.* London: Macmillan, 1975. An analysis of the forces behind British efforts to end the Atlantic slave trade, with particular attention to the intellectual background.

Aptheker, Herbert. *American Negro Slave Revolts.* 1943. Reprint, New York: International Publishers, 1963. One of the earliest attempts to document and elaborate on the prevalence of slave resistance. The author's focus is the United States.

Asiegbu, Johnson U. J. *Slavery and the Politics of Liberation, 1787–1861.* New York: Longman, Green and Co., 1969. A scholarly exploration of the Sierra Leone establishment and the contract labor from Africa that occurred after the slave trade was abolished on the Guinea Coast.

Barbot, Jean. *Barbot on Guinea: The Writings of Jean Barbot on West Africa, 1678–1712.* Edited by P. E. H. Hair, Adam Jones, and Robin Law. 2 vols. London: Hakluyt Society, 1992. A series of twenty lengthy letters, relating the author's observations on the West African coast during the era of the slave trade.

Bergad, Laird W. *The Cuban Slave Market, 1790–1880.* Cambridge Latin American Studies 79. New York: Cambridge University Press, 1995. A detailed analysis of the last major slave market in the Americas.

Bethel, Leslie. *The Abolition of the Brazilian Slave Trade.* New York: Cambridge University Press, 1970. A thorough scholarly study of the reluctant cessation of the largest and longest-lasting slave route between Africa and the New World.

Bosman, Willem. *A New and Accurate Description of the Coast of Guinea.* 1704. Reprint, New York: Barnes & Noble, 1967. A valuable primary source about Europeans in West Africa and their observations of African life and culture, with many references to the slave trade.

Buxton, Thomas Fowell. *The African Slave Trade and Its Remedy.* 1839. Reprint, London: Dawsons of Pall Mall, 1968. A nineteenth-century pro-abolitionist analysis of the African slave trade and how it should be terminated.

Clissold, Stephen. *The Barbary Slaves.* 1977. Reprint, New York: Barnes & Noble, 1992. A description of the enslavement of Europeans in North Africa during the eighteenth century.

Conrad, Robert E. *Children of God's Fire: A Documentary History of Black Slavery in Brazil.* Princeton, N.J.: Princeton University Press, 1983. A collection of primary documents, including several on the slave trade. It emphasizes the sensational aspects of the traffic and of slavery in Brazil.

Costa, Emelia Viotti da. *Crowns of Glory, Tears of Blood: The Demerara Slave Rebellion of 1823.* New York: Oxford University Press, 1994. A detailed description and analysis of one of the large slave revolts in Guyana.

Coughtry, Jay. *The Notorious Triangle: Rhode Island and the African Slave Trade, 1700–1807.* Philadelphia, Pa.: Temple University Press, 1981. The first systematic study of Rhode Island's involvement in the Atlantic slave trade.

Crosby, Alfred C., Jr. *The Columbian Exchange: Biological and Cultural Consequences of 1492.* Westport, Conn.: Greenwood Press, 1972. A study of the complex interchange of plants, animals, and germs, and their impact on the continents bordering the Atlantic.

Curtin, Philip D. *The Atlantic Slave Trade: A Census.* Madison: University of Wisconsin Press, 1969. Curtin's pioneering book set the stage for extensive research on the Atlantic slave trade. It is still a good starting point for studying the traffic.

Curtin, Philip D., ed. *Africa Remembered: Narratives by West Africans from the Era of the Slave Trade.* 2d ed. Prospect Heights, Ill.: Waveland Press, 1997. Provides access to most of the crucial narratives and recollections of slaves who were victims of the traffic and excellent information on their historical background and relative geographic locations.

Davidson, Basil. *The African Slave Trade: Precolonial History, 1450–1850.* Boston: Little, Brown Co., 1961. Published under the title *Black Mother* in 1961; prior to the extensive research on the slave trade, this narrative history was one of the few general studies available during the 1960s and 1970s.

Davies, K. G. "The Royal African Company," in *Studies in American Negro Life*. New York: Atheneum, 1970. A valuable study of an important trading firm that was deeply involved in the slave trade during the seventeenth century.

Davis, David Brion. *The Problem of Slavery in Western Culture*. Ithaca, N.Y.: Cornell University Press, 1966. This Pulitzer Prize–winning book offers an outstanding analysis of the evolution of slavery in the Western world.

———. *The Problem of Slavery in the Age of Revolution, 1770–1823*. Ithaca, N.Y.: Cornell University Press, 1975. A follow-up to *The Problem of Slavery in Western Culture,* this excellent book focuses on the gradual abolition of the slave trade and slavery during the late eighteenth and early nineteenth centuries.

Degler, Carl N. *Neither Black nor White: Slavery and Race Relations in Brazil and the United States*. New York: MacMillan, 1971. A comparative study of slavery and race relations in two societies, Brazil and the United States, that were seriously affected by slavery.

Donnan, Elisabeth. *Documents Illustrative of the Slave Trade to America*. 4 vols. Washington, D.C.: Carnegie Institution, 1930–35. An extensive and invaluable source collection. The last two volumes focus on North American and U.S. involvement in the traffic.

Drescher, Seymour. *Econocide: British Slavery in the Era of Abolition*. Pittsburgh, Pa.: University of Pittsburgh Press, 1977. A thorough and insightful analysis of economic and other motives of the slave trade.

———. *From Slavery to Freedom: Comparative Studies in the Rise and Fall of Atlantic Slavery*. New York: New York University Press, 1999. A collection of several of the author's previously published articles on the Atlantic slave trade.

Dupuis, Joseph. *Journal of a Residence in Ashantee,* with an introduction by W. E. F. Ward. 1824. Reprint, London: Frank Cass, 1966. An early nineteenth-century European reporter's account of his visit with the Asantehene on the Gold Coast (Ghana) shortly after the British ended their involvement in the slave trade.

Edwards, Paul, ed. *Equiano's Travels: The Interesting Narrative of the Life of Olaudah Equiano*. Oxford: Heinemann, 1996. A recent republication of Equiano's narrative with an extensive introduction by the editor.

Eltis, David. *Economic Growth and Ending of the Transatlantic Slave Trade*. Oxford: Oxford University Press, 1987. An excellent description and analysis of the economic implications of the slave trade during the period of abolition.

———. *The Rise of African Slavery in the Americas*. New York: Cambridge University Press, 2000. An analysis of the nature and evolution of slavery in the Americas, discussed in connection with earlier European practices of servitude.

Eltis, David, Stephen D. Behrendt, David Richardson, and Herbert S. Klein, eds. *The Trans-Atlantic Slave Trade: A Database on CD ROM.* New York: Cambridge University Press, 1999. The electronic database lists information on some 26,000 slaving voyages from all of the participating countries. It has already been used by several scholars and will continue to be an invaluable resource as upgrades make additional data available.

Eltis, David, and David Richardson, eds. *Routes to Slavery: Direction, Ethnicity and Mortality in the Atlantic Slave Trade.* London: Frank Cass, 1997. The collection of articles addresses crucial aspects of the slave trade, including one on the volume of the traffic. This is the first publication to make extensive use of the Cambridge University Press CD-ROM dataset.

Eltis, David, and James Walvin, eds. *The Abolition of the Atlantic Slave Trade.* Madison: University of Wisconsin Press, 1981. This is a multiauthor collection on a variety of slave trade topics.

Engerman, Stanley, Seymour Drescher, and Robert Paquette. *Historical Guide to World Slavery.* Oxford: Oxford University Press, 2001. This Oxford Reader contains a large variety of short selections from primary documents, from all over the world and from classical times to the present.

Engerman, Stanley L., and Eugene D. Genovese, eds. *Race and Slavery in the Western Hemisphere: Quantitative Studies.* Princeton, N.J.: Princeton University Press, 1975. One of the earliest multiauthor collections of papers on slavery and the slave trade, presented in 1972 at a conference in Rochester, New York.

Faber, Eli. *Jews, Slaves, and the Slave Trade: Setting the Record Straight.* New York: New York University Press, 1998. A scholarly analysis of allegations that Jews were disproportionately involved in the Atlantic slave trade and New World slavery.

Fogel, Robert W. *Without Consent or Contract: The Rise and Fall of American Slavery.* New York: Norton, 1989. A Nobel laureate for his work in quantitative methods, Fogel offers the most substantive analysis of slavery in North America.

Gemery, Henry A., and Jan S. Hogendorn. *The Uncommon Market: Essays on the Economic History of the Atlantic Slave Trade.* New York: Academic Press, 1979. A multiauthor collection of articles, addressing a variety of aspects of the slave trade.

Haley, Alex. *Roots: The Saga of an American Family.* New York: Doubleday, 1976. A personal saga of the author's efforts to trace his roots to Africa; later made into a television miniseries. Much of the book's depiction of the slave trade is fictional rather than historical.

Harlow, Vincent, ed. *Colonizing Expeditions to the West Indies and Guiana, 1623–1667.* Hakluyt Society, Series 2. London: Hakluyt Society, 1925.

Includes accounts of explorations, some of which shed light on the early Atlantic slave trade.

Inikori, Joseph E., and Stanley L. Engerman, eds. *The Atlantic Slave Trade: Effects on Economies, Societies, and Peoples in Africa, the Americas, and Europe.* Durham, N.C.: Duke University Press, 1992. A multiauthor collection of papers, addressing various aspects of the Atlantic slave trade.

James, C. L. R. *The Black Jacobins: Toussaint L'Ouverture and the San Domingo Revolution.* Revised edition. New York: Vintage Books, 1989. A detailed but highly eulogistic study of the life of Toussaint and his role in the successful slave revolt that led to the creation of the Republic of Haiti.

Kiple, Kenneth F. *The Caribbean Slave: A Biological History.* New York: Cambridge University Press, 1985. A study of the health conditions, morbidity, and mortality in Caribbean slave populations.

Kiple, Kenneth F., and Virginia Himmelsteib King. *Another Dimension to the Black Diaspora: Diet, Disease, and Racism.* New York: Cambridge University Press, 1981. A valuable scholarly analysis of disease transmission in the era of the slave trade.

Klein, Herbert S. *The Middle Passage: Comparative Studies in the Atlantic Slave Trade.* Princeton, N.J.: Princeton University Press, 1978. A valuable analytical study that focuses on the Middle Passage.

———. *The Atlantic Slave Trade.* New York: Cambridge University Press, 1999. An outstanding short survey and analysis of the history of the Atlantic slave trade that incorporates the most up-to-date research results, including the Cambridge University Press electronic database.

Las Casas, Bartolomé de. *The Devastation of the Indies: A Brief Account.* Translated by Herma Briffault with an introduction by Bill M. Donovan. Baltimore. Md.: Johns Hopkins University Press, 1992. A translation of Las Casas's 1522 book, with a lengthy and informative introduction discussing his controversial role in encouraging the importation of laborers from Africa.

Law, Robin. *The Slave Coast of West Africa, 1550–1750: The Impact of the African Slave Trade on an African Society.* Oxford: Oxford University Press, 1991. A scholarly study of the slave trade's impact on a specific region in Africa.

Leveen, L. Phillip. *British Slave Trade Suppression Policies, 1821–1865.* New York: Arno Press, 1977. This work concentrates on the cost the British had to pay for their efforts to end the Atlantic slave trade.

Lockhart, James, and Stuart B. Schwartz. *Early Latin America: A History of Colonial Spanish America and Brazil.* New York: Cambridge University Press, 1983. A valuable source for the demographic development of the slave populations in South and Central America.

Lovejoy, Paul. *Transformations of Slavery: A History of Slavery in Africa.* 2d ed. New York: Cambridge University Press, 2000. A penetrating scholarly

analysis of slavery in Africa and its relationship with the development of
slavery in the Americas.

Lovejoy Paul E. and Nicholas Rogers, eds. *Unfree Labour in the Development of the Atlantic World*. London: Frank Cass, 1994. A multiauthor collection of articles on various forms of forced labor in the Atlantic world.

Manning, Patrick. *Slavery in African Life: Occidental, Oriental, and African Slave Trades*. New York: Cambridge University Press, 1990. A quantitative analysis of forced migrations from Africa to Asia and the Americas, stressing African peoples and societies.

Manning, Patrick, ed. *Slave Trades, 1500–1800: Globalization of Forced Labor*. Aldershot, U.K.: Ashgate Publishing, 1996. A multiauthor collection that describes and compares slave trades to and from various global regions.

Mannix, Daniel P., and Malcolm Cowley. *Black Cargoes*. New York: Viking Press, 1962. Published before the extensive research on the slave trade since the 1970s, this narrative history was one of the few general studies available during the 1960s and 1970s.

Markham, Clements R. *The Hawkins' Voyages during the Reigns of Henry VIII, Queen Elizabeth, and James I*. Hakluyt Society, First Series. 1878. Reprint, New York: Burt Franklin Publisher, 1970. Provides evidence of sporadic English participation in the Atlantic slave trade during the sixteenth century.

Martin, Phillis M. *The External Trade of the Loango Coast, 1576–1870: The Effects of Changing Commercial Relations on the Vili Kingdom of Loango*. Oxford: Oxford University Press, 1972. A study of African merchants and their commercial relations with European slave traders.

Miers, Suzanne. *Britain and the Ending of the Slave Trade*. New York: Holmes and Meier, 1975. Analyzes the end of the British slave trade and its impact on the future of Africa.

Miers, Suzanne, and Igor Kopytoff, eds. *Slavery in Africa*. Madison: University of Wisconsin Press, 1977. This multiauthor collection explains the varieties of slavery found in Africa before and during the era of the Atlantic slave trade.

Miller, Joseph C. *Way of Death: Merchant Capitalism and the Angolan Slave Trade, 1730–1830*. Madison: University of Wisconsin Press, 1988. Winner of the Herskovits Prize, the best book on Africa that year, this is a very informative and scholarly analysis of the Atlantic slave trade in and from west-central Africa.

———. *Slavery and Slaving in World History: A Bibliography, 1900–1991*. Vol. 1. Millwood, N.Y.: Kraus International Publications, 1993.

———. *Slavery and Slaving in World History: A Bibliography, 1992–1998*. Vol. 2. Armonk, N.Y.: M.E. Sharpe, 1999. Both volumes are excellent sources for publications about the Atlantic slave trade published during the years 1900–98.

Mintz, Sidney, and Richard Price. *The Birth of African-American Culture.* Boston: Beacon Press, 1976. These anthropologists offer valuable explanations of the slave trade's impact on the formation of African American culture.

Mintz, Sidney, and Sally Price, eds. *Caribbean Contours.* Baltimore, Md.: Johns Hopkins University Press, 1983. A multiauthor publication with chapters that touch on various aspects of slavery and the slave trade in the Caribbean.

Murray, David R. *Odious Commerce: Britain, Spain, and the Abolition of the Cuban Slave Trade.* New York: Cambridge University Press, 1980. Discusses the intricate relationship between Spain, Cuba, and Britain in British efforts to end the Atlantic slave trade.

Newton, John. *Thoughts upon the African Slave Trade.* London: Buckland and Johnson, 1788. An anti-slave trade pamphlet, typical of the abolition movement during the last quarter of the eighteenth century, but written by a former slave trade captain who became a preacher as well as an abolitionist.

———. *The Journal of a Slave Trader, 1750–1754, and Thoughts upon the African Slave Trade,* ed. Bernard Martin and Mark Spurrell. London: Epsworth Press, 1962. This typical ship log of weather and currents information also provides information on the operation of the slave trade. It also includes Newton's abolitionist pamphlet against the slave trade.

Palmer, Collin A. *The First Passage: Blacks in the Americas, 1502–1617.* Oxford: Oxford University Press, 1995. A brief study of the early days of the forced immigration from Africa to the Americas.

Patterson, Orlando. *Slavery and Social Death: A Comparative Study.* Cambridge, Mass.: Harvard University Press, 1982. A sociological-historical analysis of slavery in human history by a distinguished scholar.

Phillips, William D., Jr. *Slavery from Roman Times to the Early Transatlantic Trade.* Minneapolis: University of Minnesota Press, 1985. A survey of the development of slavery from classical times to the early years of the Atlantic slave trade.

Postma, Johannes. *The Dutch in the Atlantic Slave Trade, 1600–1815.* New York: Cambridge University Press, 1990. A comprehensive survey of the Dutch involvement in the Atlantic slave trade.

Postma, Johannes, and Victor Enthoven, eds. *Riches from Atlantic Commerce: Dutch Transatlantic Trade and Shipping.* Leiden: Brill, 2003. In this multiauthor collection, several contributors focus on the Atlantic slave trade and one reassesses the Dutch slave trade.

Price, Richard. *The Guiana Maroons: A Historical and Biographical Introduction.* Baltimore, Md.: Johns Hopkins University Press, 1976. A valuable introduction to the study of maroon communities in Surinam.

Price, Richard, ed., *Maroon Societies: Rebel Slave Communities in the Americas.* 2d ed. Baltimore, Md.: Johns Hopkins University Press, 1979. A multiauthor collection about several maroon societies in the Americas.

Rawley, James A. *The Trans-Atlantic Slave Trade: A History.* New York: W.W. Norton, 1981. A general survey of the Atlantic slave trade, with special consideration for the involvement of the United States.

Richardson, David, ed. *Bristol, Africa, and the Eighteenth-Century Slave Trade to America.* 4 vols. Gloucester: A. Sutton, 1986–96. Documents of the Bristol slave trade, including the slave ship lists from that port in England.

Rodriguez, Junius P. *The Historical Encyclopedia of World Slavery.* Santa Barbara, Calif.: ABC-CLIO, 1997. Contains hundreds of short articles on various aspects of the history of slavery and the slave trade, written by specialists in selected fields.

———. *Chronology of World Slavery.* Santa Barbara, Calif.: ABC-CLIO, 1999. A very useful tool to identify important dates, events, and persons in connection with slavery and the slave trade.

Rubin, Vera, and Arthur Tuden, eds. *Comparative Perspectives on Slavery in New World Plantation Societies.* New York: Academy of Sciences, 1977. A multiauthor collection of papers about slavery and the slave trade.

Schwartz, Stuart B. *Slaves, Peasants, and Rebels: Reconsidering Brazilian Slavery.* Urbana: University of Illinois Press, 1996. A valuable source on slavery and slave rebellions in Brazil.

Solow, Barbara L., ed. *Slavery and the Rise of the Atlantic System.* New York: Cambridge University Press, 1991. A multiauthor collection of papers on various aspects of Atlantic commerce and the slave trade.

Stein, Robert L. *The French Slave Trade in the Eighteenth Century.* Madison: University of Wisconsin Press, 1979. A comprehensive survey of French involvement in the Atlantic slave trade.

Thomas, Hugh. *The Slave Trade: The Story of the Atlantic Slave Trade, 1440–1870.* New York: Simon and Schuster, 1997. A lengthy traditional narrative of the Atlantic slave trade, rich in anecdotes, especially about slave traders, but weak on scholarly analysis of the social and economic implications.

Thornton, John. *Africa and Africans in the Making of the Atlantic World, 1400–1800.* 2d ed. New York: Cambridge University Press, 1998. Especially valuable for its coverage of the African contribution to cultures surrounding the Atlantic.

Twaddle, Michael, ed. *The Wages of Slavery: From Chattel Slavery to Wage Labor in Africa, the Caribbean and England.* London: Frank Cass, 1993. A multiauthor collection of articles concerning various forms of forced labor, primarily in areas skirting the Atlantic.

Williams, Eric. *Capitalism and Slavery.* Chapel Hill: University of North Carolina Press, 1944. Stressing the economic motives for starting, maintaining, and abolishing the slave trade, this book triggered the scholarly debate over what came to be known as the "Williams Thesis."

Journal Articles

Articles about the slave trade have appeared in numerous journals and can be located through various indexes. The journals listed below publish articles on slavery and the slave trade quite regularly and can be an excellent source for further research.

American Historical Review
Bulletin of Economic Research
Economic History Review
Ethnic and Racial Studies
International History of African Historical Studies
Journal of African History
Journal of Economic History
Journal of Interdisciplinary History
Race and Slavery
Research in Economic History
Slavery and Abolition
Social Science History
William and Mary Quarterly

Occasionally, journals devote a whole issue to a specific subject. Two of these issues are especially noteworthy because all of their articles are about the Atlantic slave trade:

"La Traite des Noirs par l'Atlantique," (the Atlantic slave trade) is a special issue of the *Revue Française d'Histoire d'Outre-Mer* 62, nos. 226–27 (1975). Every article in this issue covers aspects of the Atlantic slave trade, and although the journal generally publishes in French, most of these articles are in English.

"Transoceanic Mortality: The Slave Trade in Comparative Perspective," is a special issue of the *William and Mary Quarterly* 58, no. 1 (January 2001).

This issue features only articles about the Atlantic slave trade, which were originally presented as scholarly papers at a Williamsburg, Virginia, conference in 1998.

Another crucial article that requires special attention, because it is published in a journal that rarely includes articles about the slave trade, is Georges Scelle's "The Slave Trade in the Spanish Colonies of America: The *Asiento*," *American Journal of International Law* 4 (1910): 612–61.

Films

Although several films have been made about the slave trade, they usually are biased, and more often than not they are based more on imagination than on scholarly research. Despite a few misrepresentations, however, an exception should be made for the full-length film *Amistad,* which is worth watching for its skillful dramatization. The Amistad incident also has inspired a shorter film, the *Amistad Revolt: All We Want Is to Make Us Free,* which was produced in New Haven, Connecticut, and is based on materials from the Yale archives.

The ABC miniseries *Roots: The Saga of an American Family,* based on Alex Haley's book, is worth seeing for its dramatization of the Middle Passage. One must keep in mind, however, that the film is more fiction than history and suffers from inadequate research. The BBC has produced a film for television about the life of Equiano, *A Son of Africa: The Slave Narrative of Olaudah Equiano.*

Africans have recently produced a few intriguing movies about the slave trade, including *Andagaman,* a full-length (ninety-minute) film in French and Bambara with English subtitles. It is directed by Roger Gnoan M'Bala, and is distributed by New Yorker Films. Produced in Africa by Africans, the movie is named for a fictional African king who enslaved Africans and sold them to Europeans.

For the other side of the ocean, the BBC Timewatch Series has produced a forty-seven-minute film in commemoration of Brazil's five-hundred-year history: *Brazil: An Inconvenient History.* The film stresses the important role of slavery and the slave trade in the country's history, and provides balance to the heavy emphasis that is usually placed on slavery in the United States.

The Internet provides convenient ways to learn about other films on the slave trade and slavery. See: www.ama.africatoday.com/films.htm.

Electronic Resources

One of the most important electronic tools for the slave trade is the Cambridge University Press CD-ROM slave trade dataset. It is available in many university libraries and can also be purchased from Cambridge University Press. There are many other more general electronic data resources and bibliographic tools such as World Cat, Historical Abstracts, Dissertation Abstracts, Academic Index, and Lexis/Nexis, to mention just a few, and their number is increasing. These tools are useful for locating publications, which can be printed from the computer. Most of them can be accessed through the Internet from home, but an affiliation with the providing institution may be necessary.

The Internet is another amazing tool that places nearly infinite amounts of information at our disposal. For those not yet familiar with its potential, the best way to get information on practically any subject is to employ a search engine or browser, such as Google or Alta Vista, type the subject in the search location, and push enter.

One of the big problems with the Internet, however, is that Web sites are like moving targets, they come and go or their contents change. Nevertheless, useful information on the slave trade—including films, books, conferences, and even detailed syllabi of college courses—can be obtained at several sites. If little is published about a subject, such as Sarah Margru Kinson (see biographical sketch), one can find the contents of an address about her, given by Marlene Merrill at Oberlin College, by simply searching under either of these names. See www.cc.oberlin.edu/~EOG/Kinson/Kinson.html.

A good search engine will respond to Atlantic slave trade with more suggestions than most would want to try. Some of the suggested Web sites can provide useful information, while others contain book advertisements, personal opinions, or repeating hearsay. The following may provide valuable information for further study; the first listing provides access to the Cambridge University Press slave trade dataset on CD-ROM:

www.uflib.ufl.edu/cm/history/transatlanticslavetradeguide/html;
www.unesco.org/culture/dialogue/slave/html_eng/education.shtml;
www.dpl.dacc.wisc.edu/slavetrade/index.html.

INDEX

Drought, 11, 59

Drowning, 22, 26, 90, 130, 143

Drums, 23, 25–27. *See also* Music

Dungeons, 21; Dunbomo, 103

Dupuis, Joseph, 149

Dutch Republic, 12, 15–16, 37, 52, 72, 139; its colonies, 13, 41, 43, 69; ships, 13, 26, 29, 90; slave trade, 36–37, 40, 57, 70, 78, 125, 136, 139

East Africa, 4, 40, 70

Egypt, 3–4

Elmina, 8, 26, 90, 137

Eltis, David, 12, 83

Emancipation, 73

Embarkation, 19, 21–22, 24, 45, 110, 116, 120, 124–25, 132

Emperor Charles V, 88

Encomienda, 87

England. *See* Britain

English, language, 89, 92, 100, 102, 121, 123, 125. *See also* British

Enlightenment, 63, 65, 70, 83

Enslavement, 3, 5, 11, 19, 29, 46, 55, 58–59, 71, 82, 88, 91, 100, 105–10, 117, 121. *See also* Judicial slavery

Epidemics. *See* Diseases

Equiano, Olaudah, 11, 20–21, 24, 33, 77, 89–90, 105–10, 127–31, 147–49

Essequibo, 12

Essjerrie Ettin, 29, 33, 90

Ethiopia, 4

Ethnic groups, 3, 10–11, 37–38, 80. *See also* Asante; Fante; Ibibio; Igbo; Mandinka

Evangelicals, 65–67, 92, 96, 98

Executions, 10, 29, 72, 90

Expenses in slave trade, 58, 111, 124, 138, 146; customs, 91; duties, 57–58, 125, 137–38, 140; fees, 57; insurance, 45, 51, 53, 57; presents, 57, 123–24, 137

Factor, 125, 136–37, 140. *See* Trading stations

Families, 87, 92, 98–99, 109–10, 125; fathers, 87–88, 93, 95–97, 99, 103, 105–6, 118, 121–24; sisters, 11, 77, 93, 105–8, 118; of slaves, 2, 37–38, 77, 79–80, 83, 88, 94, 103, 105, 118, 124

Famine, 11, 44, 56

Fantee, 150

Firearms, 5, 12; canon, 15, 29; guns and powder, 11, 29, 54–55, 127, 132, 142–43

Florida, 13

Fogel, Robert, 78

Food, 1, 46–47, 55, 59–60, 119, 127, 150; cassava, 59; Indian corn (maize), 24, 53, 59; malnutrition, 20, 24, 45; manioc, 59; meals, 23–24, 127; meat, 24, 53, 78; preparation, 22–24, 81, 145; provisions, 24, 45, 55, 106, 110, 113, 138, 149; rice, 13, 24, 53, 79, 144, 148; on slave ships, 24–26, 30, 45, 53, 57, 77, 106, 114; yams, 24, 46, 53. *See also* Drinking water

Forced labor, 1–2, 5, 7, 20, 81, 83, 87

France, 14, 16, 36–37, 65, 67, 69–72, 78, 92, 97–98

Free trade, 14–15, 52, 54

Freedom, 64, 84, 90, 97, 121; limited, 2, 28, 81, 94; loss of, 1, 82, 89; regained, 9, 30, 58, 69, 73, 88–89, 92, 95, 121, 124

Freetown, 71, 100–104, 117

French: abolitionists, 65, 71; colonies, 12, 41, 43, 65, 69, 97,

Methodists, 65–66, 96, 100

Mexico, 41, 78, 88

Middelburg, 144

Middelburgs Welvaren, 29

Middle Ages, 3, 5, 64

Middle East, 2, 5, 46

Middle Passage, 19, 21–22, 24–27, 33, 35, 43–44, 47, 57, 68, 71, 77, 90, 127–31, 147; survival, 26, 29, 44, 47, 58, 80, 116; transshipment, 6, 41, 120–21. *See also* Diseases

Middle Passage slave confinement: chains, 22–23, 92, 112, 118–20, 127–30, 133; crowding, 23, 25, 45, 129; deck space, 22–24, 26–27, 29, 47, 94, 127, 136, 142–43, 147; exercise, 24; fetters, 112, 119, 121, 127, 130; irons, 110–13, 116, 120, 130, 133, 136, 141, 143; platforms, 23, 135; shackles, 23, 27; stench, 22, 130, 136; suffocation, 26, 120, 129–30; tight packing, 45

Migration, 1, 4, 17, 33, 46

Miller, Joseph, 20–21, 55, 59

Minas Gerais, 9, 41

Mines, 3, 8–9, 36, 41

Missionary activities, 71, 79, 100–104, 117

Mississippi, 79

Modern values, 83

Mohamedan. *See* Muslims

Money, 52, 89, 102–3, 108, 124, 126, 132, 146; currencies, 54, 56

Monopolies, 8, 14

Monrovia, 71

Montague (Duke of), 93–94, 125

Montes, Pedro, 101–3

Moors, 3, 9

Morocco, 4

Mortality, 8, 14, 21, 29–30, 33, 35, 44–45, 51, 56–57, 59, 78–79, 82, 95; in Africa, 21, 59; on Middle Passage, 24, 26, 35, 40, 43–59, 71. *See also* Crew mortality

Moses, 80

Mozambique, 40

Mulattos, 78, 97

Music: gospel, 81, 94; jazz, 81; Negro spirituals, 80–81. *See also* Drums

Muslims, 3, 10, 88, 118, 121, 123, 149–50

Mutinies, 135

Myrmidon, 120

Napoleon, Napoleonic Empire, 52, 69–70, 97

Nat Turner's revolt, 69

Nazi racism, 82

Negro spirituals. *See* Music

Neptunis, 29

Netherlands. *See* Dutch Republic

New England, 15, 51, 91

New Granada, 93, 95

New Haven, 102–3

New World, 9, 11, 19, 31, 40, 43, 46, 77–78, 80, 87, 93, 119. *See also* Western Hemisphere

New World slavery, 65, 81–82. *See also* Race, racism

New York, 67, 102

Newton, John, 27, 33, 66, 95–96, 131–36

Niger: delta, 15; mission, 101; river 13, 101, 110–11, 150

Nigeria, 10, 16, 71, 89, 100–101, 105, 117

Noble savage, 64

North Africa, 2–4, 27, 46

Nwokeji, Ugo, 46

About the Author

JOHANNES POSTMA is Professor of History at Minnesota State University and the author of *The Dutch in the Atlantic Slave Trade, 1600–1815*, among other works.